***Another Look
At The Lord's Prayer***

Abba

Ron Lavin

CSS Publishing Company, Inc., Lima, Ohio

ABBA

Copyright © 2002 by
CSS Publishing Company, Inc.
Lima, Ohio

All rights reserved. No part of this publication may be reproduced in any manner whatsoever without the prior permission of the publisher, except in the case of brief quotations embodied in critical articles and reviews. Inquiries should be addressed to: Permissions, CSS Publishing Company, Inc., P.O. Box 4503, Lima, Ohio 45802-4503.

Unless otherwise marked, Scripture quotations are taken from the *Holy Bible, New International Version*. Copyright © 1973, 1978, 1984 International Bible Society. Used by permission of Zondervan Bible Publishers. All rights reserved.

Scripture quotations marked (RSV) are from the *Revised Standard Version of the Bible*, copyrighted 1946, 1952 ©, 1971, 1973, by the Division of Christian Education of the National Council of the Churches of Christ in the USA. Used by permission.

Library of Congress Cataloging-in-Publication Data

Lavin, Ronald J.
  Abba : another look at the Lord's prayer / Ron Lavin.
    p. cm.
  ISBN 0-7880-1940-6
  1. Lord's prayer. I. Title.
  BV230 .L3832 2003
  226.9'606—dc21

2002013914

For more information about CSS Publishing Company resources, visit our website at www.csspub.com or e-mail us at custserv@csspub.com or call (800) 241-4056.

ISBN 0-7880-1940-6   PRINTED IN U.S.A.

This book is dedicated to
Harry and Dodie Andersen
and
Carol Lewis

Books By Ron Lavin

The *Another Look* Series
I Believe; Help My Unbelief: Another Look At The Apostles' Creed
Stories To Remember: Another Look At The Parables Of Jesus
Abba: Another Look At The Lord's Prayer

To be published soon:
The Big Ten: Another Look At The Ten Commandments
Saving Grace: Another Look At The Sacraments

Other Books In Print
Turning Griping Into Gratitude
Empty Spaces; Empty Places (written with Constance Sorenson)
Way To Grow!
The Advocate
The Great I AM
Previews Of Coming Attractions

Previously Published Books
Alone / Together
You Can't Start A Car With A Cross
You Can Grow In A Small Group
Jesus In Stained Glass
Jesus Christ, The Liberator (written with Bill Grimmer, MD)
Hey, Mom, Look At Me!

The Lord's Prayer
Contemporary Version

Our Father in heaven
   hallowed be your name,
   your kingdom come,
   your will be done,
      on earth as in heaven
Give us today our daily bread.
Forgive us our sins
   as we forgive those
      who sin against us.
Save us from the time of trial
   and deliver us from evil.
For the kingdom, the power,
   and the glory are yours
   now and forever. Amen.

The Lord's Prayer
Traditional Version

Our Father, who art in heaven,
   hallowed be thy name,
   thy kingdom come,
   thy will be done,
      on earth as it is in heaven.
Give us this day our daily bread;
and forgive us our trespasses,
   as we forgive those
      who trespass against us;
and lead us not into temptation,
   but deliver us from evil,
For thine is the kingdom,
   and the power, and the glory,
   forever and ever. Amen.

Table Of Contents

Preface by Melvin M. Kieschnick	9
Introduction	11
Books In The "Another Look" Series	19
1. Our Father	21
2. Heaven And God's Hallowed Name	29
3. Your Kingdom Come	37
4. Your Will Be Done On Earth As It Is In Heaven	43
5. Give Us Tomorrow's Bread Today	49
6. Forgive Us	55
7. Save Us From The Great Ordeal And Deliver Us From The Evil One	69
8. Your Glory	79
Endnotes	89
Tips For Teachers, Pastors, And Leaders	91

Appendix #1
    A Mother's View Of The Lord's Prayer
    by Mary Lavin Cousler
	93

Appendix #2 My Journey by Carol Lewis	99

Preface

By Melvin M. Kieschnick
Former Director of Parish Education
The Lutheran Church — Missouri Synod

In spite of the growth of both ancient and new age spirituality, the Lord's Prayer most likely continues to be the world's most widely prayed litany of petition and praise. This reality creates the potential for the prayer to be said by rote and routine so that its deep spiritual yearnings may lose their power and depth. In this thoughtful book on the Lord's Prayer, Ron Lavin brings into focus both traditional teachings and new insights which can help anyone praying or studying this prayer of our Lord to gain deeper meaning. Written from the heart of a parish pastor, and with keen insights of a thoughtful theologian, this book illuminates both the heart and mind of the reader.

Drawing heavily on the concept of the kingdom of God, Lavin examines each portion of the Lord's Prayer uniting the theological and practical dimensions of this timeless supplication. One example is the way in which the traditional, "Give us today our daily bread," is given fresh and new vigor when articulated, "Give us tomorrow's bread today."

Lavin's pastoral ministry is heavily reflected in his use of memorable stories of ordinary and extraordinary parishioners whose struggles and triumphs are illustrated in the understandings of these petitions. Further, the interpretation given to the various portions of the prayer demonstrate how the Lord's Prayer is both individual and corporate. The one who prays, prays not only for himself, but for the world.

Abba is an appreciated resource for personal meditation, a sermon series, and group discussion. It can help all who pray the prayer our Lord taught us.

Introduction

In 1975 I was named Pastor-Director of Evangelical Outreach for the Lutheran Church in America. At that time I gave a lot of thought to the connection between evangelical outreach and prayer, especially the Lord's Prayer. What does prayer have to do with people coming to faith in Jesus Christ? How is the Lord's Prayer related to evangelical outreach to the unchurched? What was Jesus really teaching the first disciples about prayer and witness? What is the link between the kingdom of God, evangelism, and the Lord's Prayer? These questions were on my mind as I lectured and preached around the country between 1975 and 1988.

In 1988, the content of this book, *Abba, Another Look At The Lord's Prayer*, began to formulate in my mind when I was on study leave from parish ministry in Canterbury, England. There I studied under Dr. John V. Taylor, the Anglican missionary and Bishop who wrote *The Go-between God*, a wonderful book on the Holy Spirit. Dr. Taylor's lectures were on "The Kingdom of God and the Lord's Prayer." "This," I thought in advance, "will be a great chance to learn from someone I respect for his book about the Holy Spirit." His topic was of great interest to me since both of the topics were closely related to my work as a pastor and an evangelist.

When Dr. Taylor stood and walked to the pulpit of the chapel of King's College where we met, I thought to myself, "Maybe I made a mistake." He was retired now, it was announced. "Maybe he had lost his edge as a presenter," I thought. Then I noticed that he had forgotten to put his clergy collar on that morning. I had had a forgetful seminary professor like that who was "over the hill" which made me ponder, "I have traveled a long distance. Maybe this will not be worthwhile." I believe in eye contact for preachers and lecturers. When Dr. Taylor started to read his manuscript, with very little eye contact, I thought that I had made a serious mistake.

I was wrong. For five days I was enthralled by the wise words from the old bishop-theologian about the kingdom of God and the Lord's Prayer. Both topics were of vital interest to me. Taylor took a fresh approach to both topics. He said, "Not only is the petition

'Your kingdom come' about the kingdom of God; everything in the Lord's Prayer is about the kingdom of God. Without understanding the kingdom of God, you cannot really understand the prayer of Jesus. As a matter of fact, you cannot understand the Bible without understanding the centrality of the kingdom of God. The kingdom of God is God's reign over us, his rule, his authority. The kingdom of God is central to the Bible and to Jesus' prayer."

Dr. Taylor went on to explain what I knew but had not connected to the Lord's Prayer before this time. "When Jesus came, the kingdom broke into human life. In Jesus, the kingdom did not come in its perfection; that will only happen at the end of time, but he ushered in the kingdom and more importantly, he expected his followers to start living now as if the kingdom had arrived. It hasn't arrived yet; it has only approached, but Jesus expected us to live as if it had arrived. That is what the Lord's Prayer is all about. Yes, that is what Jesus had in mind as he taught his disciples to pray."

When Jesus prayed to his Father in the words we call the Lord's Prayer, he was teaching the first disciple how to pray and how to live. He taught them that we live in the time between his first and his second coming.

My mind was filled with memories of what I had heard and read in seminary and beyond about the Lord's reign in our lives. I also remembered something about living between the first and second comings of Christ. Some theologian, I do not remember who it was, had described the times between the first and second coming of the Lord like this: "We now live between the lightning and the thunder. When we see the one, we know that the other is coming. We wait with great anticipation." I thought, "Yes, that's what Dr. Taylor is saying. When you know what is coming, you live in the sure and certain hope of God's reign over his creation. When you see the lightning, you know that the thunder will come soon, and if you know that, you must get to people who don't know about the kingdom with the message that they'd better be ready because the Lord is coming soon."

"The Lord's Prayer is all about the coming of the kingdom of God," Dr. Taylor repeated. Then he went on to explain each word and phrase in the light of the kingdom of God. For example, *Abba*, an Aramaic word, is the first word of the Lord's Prayer in Luke 11:1-2. Aramaic, a dialect of the Hebrew language, is one of the languages Jesus used. *Abba means Daddy.* The first word in the Lord's Prayer, is about what the kingdom of God means: affectionate intimacy with the Ruler of the universe. This is what Jesus ushered in as the kingdom of God approached in his coming. This is a kingdom where the King loves the subjects so personally that he wants them to call him "Daddy."

"Abba, your name is holy." Think of it. We know the eternal King intimately through Jesus Christ. The King is holy. His name is holy. If the kingdom of God has broken in through Jesus Christ, and if we are called to live as citizens of heaven now, then how we spend our time and money, how we set our priorities and goals, how we live our lives — all of this and more — is involved in praying the Lord's Prayer.

"Your kingdom come" is a petition about the second coming of Christ. Of course we want him to come soon. Of course we want to be ready. Of course we want others to be ready. As I thought about this petition of the Lord's Prayer, the implications for evangelical outreach were stunning.

"Your kingdom come" is about the hereafter. It is about heaven and God's desire that we live with him forever.

"Your kingdom come" is also about the here and now. The kingdom of God came when Jesus came. The kingdom of God will come at the end of time. The kingdom of God also comes now as we come to faith in Christ.

"Your will be done on earth as it is in heaven." This petition too is about the kingdom of God. Isn't doing the will of God what the kingdom of God is all about? Gladly and joyously doing our Abba's will is the nature of the love we give back to the one who loved us first.

"Give us today our daily bread." How could asking God for food for the table be a part of the kingdom of God? Dr. Taylor suggested the seed thought for the connection between bread and kingdom when he said, "Alternatively, the translation of this verse is 'Give us tomorrow's bread today.' " I had read this earlier, but the implications dawned on me one day in Canterbury, England, when I heard it as if I had never heard it before. I thought, "Tomorrow's bread is the bread which comes from heaven, the manna for the wilderness wanderers on the way to the Promised Land. This bread from heaven strengthens us for the journey through life as the kingdom of God people."

"Forgive us our sins as we forgive those who sin against us." Forgiveness is the heart of the matter for the kingdom of God people on the journey through life. By the power of God, not our human effort, but *the power of God*, we can forgive our enemies, just as Jesus did. If we are living between the lightning and the thunder, we can offer forgiveness to those who hurt us, *even when they don't deserve it, even if they don't ask for it, even if they do not repent.* We can do this as Jesus did it, not of ourselves, but by the indwelling of God's Holy Spirit in us. Since we Christians are both sinners and saints, we will not forgive perfectly. We will sometimes forget our Lord's way, but when we pray the Lord's Prayer petition about forgiveness we will be reminded what life is really supposed to be like. When we treat people as Jesus did, they will sometimes wake up to the reality of God. When we reflect on what has been done to us and for us in Jesus Christ when we were not worthy recipients of forgiveness, we can pass on forgiveness to others, *even when in our estimation they do not deserve it.*

Admittedly, we do not have the full picture of what this profound petition means. Admittedly, we see only through a glass darkly. But as we pray this petition, we see something, a fleeting image of how to treat others as we have been treated by God, a preview of coming attractions. The Greek word in the New Testament for this preview is *arroban. Arroban* literally means "down payment." We get a down payment of heavenly ways when we live as we pray in this petition.

"Lead us not into temptation" is the traditional translation of the next phrase in the Lord's Prayer. I had always felt that this was a strange petition. God does not lead us into temptation. God tempts no one to sin. Temptation is the business of the Tempter.

An alternate translation, "Save us from the Great Ordeal," may be closer to what Jesus had in mind when he prayed this prayer and taught his disciples to pray it. Dr. Taylor suggested that the meaning of the Great Ordeal is best understood in the light of Jesus' cry from the cross, "My God, my God, why have you forsaken me?" This was Jesus' dark night of the soul when it seemed that even his Abba had forgotten and forsaken him. This is the dark night of the soul which many of God's saints have experienced. They have had a close, intimate relationship with Abba, when suddenly, seemingly out of nowhere, the Tempter fills them with thoughts that they are alone, that their Father just doesn't care any more. This is the dark night of the soul which we pray we will never experience. This is the Great Ordeal.

We pray, "Save us from the Great Ordeal, and deliver us from the Evil One," because this Great Ordeal is the one thing above everything else to be avoided. God does not forsake us, but *there are times when it seems that even you, our Abba, have left us, times when we need you the most, times of ultimate temptation when the Evil One seems to be in control. Abba, please save us from these times and if they come, bring us back to your tender, loving care.*

"For yours is the kingdom, the glory and the power," we pray at the end of the Lord's Prayer. This doxology was probably added later, but it certainly fits the theme of the kingdom of God and God's reign in our lives.

God's reign. Yes, that is what the Lord's Prayer is all about. That link between Jesus' prayer and the kingdom of God dawned on me in the summer of 1988 when I heard Dr. John V. Taylor speak.

God's reign. Yes, that is what evangelical outreach is all about, reestablishing God's reign over a person's life for his or her own good. When we were born, we were intended to come under Abba's loving reign. Jesus made this return to God's rule possible through his death on the cross.

God's reign. Yes, that is the only way to avoid the reign of someone or something else which will only destroy us. Luther observed that like a horse we are either ridden by God, the rider, or we are ridden by the Devil. That is what both the Lord's Prayer and evangelical outreach are all about. An anonymous author put it this way:

> *Unless that which is above you controls*
> *that which is within you,*
> *then that which around you*
> *will.*

Since 1988, I have been working on this book about God's reign and the Lord's Prayer. I am indebted to many mentors in the faith who have refined my concepts and connections. Theological mentors John V. Taylor, George Forell, Pat Keifert, and Bill Lazareth have all helped refine my ideas. If an idea is clear to you, the reader, one of them is probably the contributor. If an idea is unclear, I take full responsibility.

Lay men and women of all ages have also served as guides, not only in the area of concepts and theological connections, but in the all-important area of practice. It is one thing to get an idea right; it is quite another to live it right. Many of these guides in practical theology are mentioned in my book, *The Advocate* (CSS, 1999). Three are singled out here for special mention. This book is dedicated to these three special people.

Harry Andersen, the president of King of Glory Lutheran Church in Fountain Valley, California, when I became the senior pastor there in 1993, embodies many of the qualities of the kingdom-of-God Christian who lives *in* but is not *of* the world. Harry died of cancer in 1999. He gave me many previews of coming attractions. Just before he died, he gave me a special preview of heaven. In heaven, there will be singing and dancing. There will also be laughter. On his death bed, Harry told me this story:

A man was dying of cancer (just as Harry was). This man was unable to get out of his bed which was on the second floor of his house. One day he smelled chocolate chip cookies (his favorites) baking in the kitchen downstairs. He had to have one. He called for his wife, but she didn't hear him. He rolled out of bed, painfully crawled down the steps and into the kitchen. When he reached up to the table top to get a cookie, his wife — who had just come in from outside — slapped his hand with a spatula.

"Why did you do that?" he moaned.

"Those cookies are for your funeral reception," she replied.

Harry and his wife Dodie (the second special person to whom this book is dedicated) laughed so hard they cried as they told me that story. I doubled up and rolled on the floor. When you can laugh at bony Death, you have won the battle with him. When you laugh at Death, you are a kingdom-of-God man or woman. Thanks, Harry and Dodie. This book's for you.

This book is also dedicated to Carol Lewis. Carol is a good example of someone who had a dysfunctional father and was about to step off the edge of a dangerous cliff, when suddenly Abba stepped in and changed her thinking. You will meet her in chapter one of this book. (Note to the reader: You may want to read Carol's story in Appendix #2 in the back of the book, before reading chapter 1.) Carol, for all you do (and more importantly, what God has done for you), this book's for you.

Lay people have taught me a lot about what it means to have an Abba and be kingdom-of-God people. Many people deserve my thanks for contributions they have made to the writing of this book. Let me mention just nine.

Susan Kiddy, my secretary, typed the final draft of this manuscript a month before her fatal heart attack. She made many helpful suggestions and changes in the manuscript. Don McMillan, my associate pastor for many years, was a loyal partner and is a friend whose pastoral care is a good example of how Abba works in life.

Bud Potter, who heads up "Go and Do Likewise" at King of Glory Lutheran Church in Fountain Valley, California, leads a group which goes out into the community each month painting houses, cutting down or trimming trees and bushes, fixing cars, or doing other fix-up work for widows, single women, and other needy people who cannot do this work for themselves or pay for someone else to do it. This work is all done free with no strings attached for many unchurched people in and around Fountain Valley, California. This selfless service is a preview of heaven, a way to put the Lord's Prayer into action. Many who have received this service comment, "I can't believe that you have done all this work for me for free."

In addition, I owe a debt of gratitude to Pete Moenter, Dale Siegele, and Rod and Caroline Anderson, who have contributed insights to this book. Mel Kieschnick co-taught a course on the Lord's Prayer with me at Calvary Lutheran Church in Solana Beach, California, where we both learned a lot from the class members. Tom Lentz, the former Acquisition Editor at CSS Publishing, has been a great encourager in the production of all my CSS books. Thank you, one and all, for insights that led to the writing of this book.

Abba is our strong, dependable Father. But he is also compassionate and loving. Time and again he shows us what Brennan Manning calls "relentless tenderness." This relentless tenderness is best symbolized in a mother with a new-born baby. Children learn both strength and tenderness from Christian mothers and fathers. Family is the context for Jesus using the word "Abba" for God. For that reason, there is an Appendix in this book about children. It is written by my daughter Mary Lavin Cousler. Appendix #1, "A Mother's View Of The Lord's Prayer," places the Lord's Prayer in the context of family. This Appendix "humanizes" Jesus' prayer in a way that may be helpful to you. You may want to read it before reading the book.

Pastors, teachers, and small group leaders should check the section called "Tips For Teachers, Pastors, And Leaders" in the back of this book.

Most of the biblical quotations in this book are from the *New International Version* (NIV). Other translations, including the *Revised Standard Version*, are noted where they are used.

Writing *Abba* has brought me many blessings. To you, the reader, I offer my best wishes for a good journey into the Lord's Prayer and most importantly for your life journey with our Abba.

    Ron Lavin
    E-mail for speaking engagements
    randjlavin@cox.net
    Encinitas, California

Books In The "Another Look" Series

Abba is the third book in the "Another Look" series. The previous two are *I Believe; Help My Unbelief* (about the Apostles' Creed, CSS, 2001) and *Stories To Remember* (about the parables of Jesus, CSS, 2002). *Saving Grace* (about the Word and Sacraments) and *The Big Ten* (about the Ten Commandments) will be published in the near future. All of the books in this series are about getting back to basics and going forward with basics.

In the morass of ideas and philosophies today, many people drift away from Christian basics. The "Another Look" series is a call to get back to the faith fundamentals that have sustained our forefathers and foremothers. But this series is also a call to go forward with the basics. How can we go forward without them? Aren't we just fooling ourselves when we cling to New Age religion or the wide variety of heresies offered to us on a daily basis? Will idolatry ever work for our good?

The books in this series are for individual study and inspiration. They are also for adult Sunday school classes, pastor's classes, sermon preparation, Bible study groups, prayer groups, or koinonia (fellowship) groups meeting in homes or churches. Questions at the end of each chapter encourage discussion. For individuals, classes, and groups, blessings for your study of the prayer that changes the way we look at God, ourselves, our present, and our future.

Chapter 1

Our Father

He (Jesus) was praying in a certain place, and when he ceased, one of his disciples said to him, "Lord, teach us to pray, as John taught his disciples." And he said to them, "When you pray, say: Father...."
— Luke 11:1-2

* * *

A young woman named Carol discovered her status as a child of the heavenly Father, in spite of the fact that her earthly father was not much of a father. When our family first met Carol in Lebanon, Indiana, she was a fourteen-year-old unchurched teenager with a "devil-may-care" attitude. When she started coming to church, our first church out of seminary, Carol brought her sense of humor along with her. She called me "Pastor Baby." Much of the humor was a cover-up. Carol had serious problems.

Carol's biggest problem was that she felt inadequate. Her father was an alcoholic. She had a brother and a brother-in-law who were in prison. It appeared that Carol would also be destined to become a nonproductive liability in society. Her destiny seemed sealed when her father committed suicide and left the family destitute.

Instead, as a teenager, Carol met God, our heavenly Father, and her sense of worth began to rise. When it came time for college, our family encouraged Carol to attend Ball State University in Muncie, Indiana, where I was a pastor at Holy Trinity Church. "I can't," she said. "Why?" my wife Joyce and I inquired. She replied, "There are two reasons: 1) I'm too dumb and 2) I don't have any money."

"You're not too dumb," we said. "If we get the money for you, will you try it?"

"Yes," she said, "but it won't work."

One of our neighbors worked in the Scholarship Department of Ball State University. We asked for scholarship help for Carol. She got it. Two members of our church, Dr. and Mrs. Sam Dry, both professors at the University, said that Carol could have free room and board at their home for watching their two children. Carol came to college on a hope and a prayer. She had just $20.00 to her name when she arrived. Through hard work, faith in God, and the generosity of Christian friends, she finished college. Today Carol is a teacher of the deaf in St. Augustine, Florida. All this happened because she made the ultimate discovery that God is our heavenly Father. For Carol the discovery that God was her Father had several stops and starts, but it was a life-changing discovery. It is for everyone. All of life is a search for our Father.

My Abba

Jesus used the Aramaic term *Abba*, when he was asked by his disciples how to pray. "When you pray, say, *Abba*," he said. This was the familiar term of affectionate intimacy used by Jesus every time he prayed, with one exception. The one exception is the cry of dereliction from the cross, "My God, my God, why have you forsaken me?" In every prayer but this one, Jesus calls God, *Abba*.

Abba is the term used by a Jewish boy or girl personally addressing his or her father. As far as we know, no religious leader before Jesus ever suggested that we should address God in such a familiar and affectionate way. Since God is holy, this term seemed overly familiar to his contemporaries, but Jesus was showing them and us the way of real prayer. In the Lord's Prayer, Jesus is not only teaching us how to pray. This is how he prayed. First and foremost, the Lord's Prayer is Jesus' prayer. He prayed, "Abba." Only then did he teach his disciples to pray this personal way.

"Abba" can only be spoken appropriately by a child. If you are not a child of God, you cannot pray "Abba." But, of course, God sees you as his child. He wants you to pray this way. He invites you to pray this way. Jesus shows you how to pray this way.

A story may help to drive this point home. Jesus often used stories of participation to help his hearers grasp the seemingly unfathomable truths of the kingdom of God. That we can and should call God, "Our Daddy," is one of those unfathomable truths which may be best carried by a story.

A little boy was waving at a big paddle boat on the Mississippi River. He was motioning for the captain to bring the boat to shore where he was standing. A passerby chuckled and said, "Son, that big paddle boat will never come to shore here. Your waving is in vain." Just then, the big paddle boat turned sharply toward the spot where the little boy was waving. The little boy looked up at the stranger and through several missing teeth in front said, "The captain is my daddy."

Something like that is going on as we begin the Lord's Prayer. The Captain of the universe turns toward us when he sees our wave and hears our plea, "Daddy, come here."

That God is our heavenly Father is the theme of the prayer which Jesus taught his disciples to pray. The disciples said, "Teach us to pray." "When you pray," Jesus replied, "say 'Abba.'" "Abba" is a personal greeting. If we really believed that we could talk to God personally, we would have much less difficulty with prayer.

Many people, even many active church members, feel very inadequate when it comes to prayer. Perhaps one of the reasons for this is that they have heard pastors and priests pray publicly, using big words or fancy phrases and they feel that they cannot speak with God that way. "Not necessary," Jesus said, "just say, 'Abba.'" Feel inadequate? Just say, "Daddy."

As we begin this journey into the Lord's Prayer, we can be encouraged by the fact that like us, the apostles felt inadequate in prayer. The presenting problem which led to the Lord giving this prayer was that his followers said, "Lord, teach us to pray."

Notice that Jesus answers this request by *showing*, not telling. Jesus' common means of teaching is to show, not tell. Showing implies involvement, not merely observation. Jesus did not give a detailed list of instructions on prayer. He prayed. He set the pattern of prayer by calling God, "Abba."

Since the Lord taught us to pray beginning with the simple childlike greeting, "Abba," we are encouraged to use simple, personal ways of approaching God in prayer. In his *Small Catechism*, Martin Luther says that the obvious conclusion of this beginning is that we are God's children. As such, we can talk with God about anything that is on our minds and hearts, no matter how small our needs may be, no matter how poorly put our petitions may be. The Lord's Prayer is highly personal. It is also communal.

Our Abba

In Matthew 6:9, the parallel passage to Luke 11:1-2, the Lord's Prayer starts, "Our Father ..." adding the community dimension to this highly personal prayer.

To be sure, God is *the* Father of the universe, the creator of all things in heaven and earth. That is true enough, but not personal enough. God is also *my* Father, personally interested in me as if there was no other person on the face of the earth. That is personal enough, but not communal enough. The heart of prayer is dealt with when we begin, "*Our* Father." We pray as part of the community of faith. There are at least two implications to this greeting.

First, when Jesus prayed "Our Father," he was teaching us something about our enemies, those who hurt us or hate us. "Love your enemies," Jesus said. That means that we should not pray against anyone. We may try to bring revenge into our prayers saying, "Look what he did to me, Father ... Now punish ..." But if we draw close to God in prayer, he will soon have us praying *for* our enemies instead of *against* them.

A little boy once said to his pastor, "If I pray with my hands pointed up or out that means that I am praying *for* someone. Right?" "Yes," said the pastor. "When I pray with my hands pointed down, does that mean that I can pray *against* someone who hurt me?" "No," said the pastor. "When we pray 'Our Father,' that eliminates praying against anyone."

A farmer once poisoned the pond of his neighbor whom he hated. The next day when he looked out he saw that all his neighbor's cattle were dead. But his own cattle were dead too. There was a secret underground tunnel from his neighbor's pond which led to his own. We are secretly linked to all our neighbors. Thus we pray, "Our Father."

Second, if God is *our* Father, that means that you are my sister or brother. I cannot have the one without the other. We may be different people with different styles and ideas, but once baptized, we are family. Whether we like it or not, agree with it or not, accept it or not, we are brothers and sisters. Period. We are family. Period. That means that we are called to love one another and work together for the glory of God.

"*Our* Father" means that the stark, raving, individualistic religion which asserts, "I can have *my own* religion, and do *my own* thing, in *my own way*" is an expression of one of the most serious problems we have in what has been called the "Me Generation." The biblical corrective for too much *me* in religion and in life is the greeting of the Lord's Prayer, "*Our* Father."

Jesus' introduction to prayer is both highly personal and emphatically communal. The story of Gert Behanna may help to drive this point home.

Gert Behanna's father was a millionaire with lots of high, unrealistic expectations for her. He showed her little love. Gert did not have the good looks of her mother, nor the brains of her father. She was a disappointment in every way. She turned to alcohol after two failed marriages. An alcoholic who was hooked on amphetamines and barbiturates, Gert tried suicide. When she awakened in the hospital with life-supporting devices in every direction, she realized that she could not even succeed in taking her own life. An attending physician told her, "You are a very sick woman and there is nothing wrong with you. I am going to send you to a psychiatrist."

"I don't need a psychiatrist," Gert said. "I need God."

In her book *The Late Liz* (and the movie by the same title starring Anne Baxter), Gert says that she doesn't know where that idea of turning to God came from because for the first fifty years of her life she knew no one who said he or she believed in God. After failing to take her own life, Gert visited a friend who introduced her to some Christians. In order to talk to her first Christians, Gert got drunk. "That," she said later, "is not so much a commentary on us drunks as on us Christians. If someone has to get drunk to meet a Christian, something is wrong somewhere."

Her friends said, "Gert, why don't you turn your troubles over to God?"

"Just like that?" she asked.

"Yes," they said, "just like that."

"Like a porter carrying my luggage?"

"Yes," they said, "something like that." They let her have God at a level she understood — a porter. Gert calls this "the courtesy of Christ." Christ will start with us wherever we are.

When Gert got home she received a letter from her new Christian friends and an article by Sam Shoemaker titled "How to Become a Christian." This article spoke to her about Jesus, her brother, and God, her Father. These friends cared. They really cared. In the context of Christian caring, Gert turned her life over to God.

When Gert turned her life over to God, the first thing she did was try to pray. On her knees for the first time in her life, she recalled the only prayer she had ever heard: "Our Father ..." she began. Then she paused and was overwhelmed by the thought: "Our Father ..." "That means protection and love from God, our real Father." That means that all believers are together in one family. I, who had never really known a loving father — only a demanding one — and had never really had any brothers or sisters and no real friends — only acquaintances — now suddenly had God for a Father and Christians all over the world as brothers and sisters.

That's it! That's what millions have discovered. We have a loving heavenly Father and Christian brothers and sisters everywhere. That is the greatest discovery in the world! To be converted means that we awaken as from a long sleep to the reality that God is our *Abba*. We then trust or commit ourselves to this Daddy like a little boy or girl puts his or her hand in the hand of his or her daddy crossing a busy street. Then we take the hands of others and call them family since they are our brothers and sisters.

We have a heavenly Father! Jesus called him "Abba." When we have had bad experiences with fathers or family or other human beings, it seems almost impossible to trust God. To trust God may be the hardest thing of all, but it is the one thing needful. When we learn to trust God as our *Abba*, we are experiencing the miracle of the kingdom of God, with God as our Father and other Christians as our brothers and sisters.

Questions And Ideas
For Your Consideration And Discussion

1. When did you first learn the Lord's Prayer? Who taught you?

2. In praying the Lord's Prayer, what difference does it make that people have had good or bad experiences with their earthly fathers?

3. How do we help people overcome any bad family experiences they have had which inhibits their ability to pray the Lord's Prayer?

4. What is the danger in just saying the Lord's Prayer instead of praying it?

5. Comment on the conversion experiences of Carol Lewis and Gert Behanna in this chapter.

6. If you haven't already done so, go to Appendix #2 in this book and read the story of Carol's faith journey as she describes it.

Chapter 2

Heaven And God's Hallowed Name

> *This, then, is how you should pray: "Our Father in heaven, hallowed be your name ..."*
> — Matthew 6:9

* * *

In the Lord's Prayer, we speak to God as our *Abba*, our daddy. But note that this Father we address is our *heavenly* Father. In other words, God is perfect, unlike our earthly fathers. Even if our earthly fathers are very good, they are imperfect and sinful. God is holy.

In the first petition of the Lord's Prayer, "Hallowed be your name," we confess not only that God is holy; we also confess that God's name is holy. Martin Luther puts it this way in *The Small Catechism*:

> *God's name certainly is holy in itself, but we ask in this prayer that we may keep it holy.*[1]

In other words, we are praying to the holy God who has a holy name, and we pray that we may keep this God and his name holy in our lives. Let us start with the holy God, our heavenly Father.

Heaven — The Hereafter And The Here And Now

In a materialistic and secular world, it never ceases to amaze me how interested people are in the topic of heaven. Some years ago when I spoke at a service club, one of the men asked to talk to me afterward. He said, "Do you believe in heaven for this life or the next?" My response was: "Yes." "Yes?" he asked. "Yes," I said, "because heaven is for the here and now and the hereafter, not one or the other. Heaven begins here through faith in Jesus Christ even while we are sinners. We experience heaven in its perfection in the hereafter."

People are fascinated with the topic of heaven. Books about after-death experiences are popular. While there are many distortions in the popularization of heavenly matters, the point is that people really have questions about and interest in heaven, even though many live as if there is only today.

There is much confusion about heaven. When we pray, "Our Father in heaven," we don't mean that God is off in the celestial clouds, 100,000 miles beyond the moon. When we say, "Our heavenly Father," we are not saying that we believe in a God who is located on Cloud 22.

God is not off in the heavens like some super Santa Claus. He is heavenly in the sense that he is perfect, beyond measure, high and holy. In addition to being perfect, beyond measure, and high and holy, this heavenly Father brings eternity to earth. He adds a heavenly dimension to all he touches. The kingdom of God can break into people's lives not only in the hereafter but in the here and now.

Jesus taught us to pray, "Our Father in heaven." What did he mean? Dr. George Forell, a Lutheran theologian, in a lecture on the Lord's Prayer, said that many people have pressing questions about heaven. "What is heaven like?" he asked. "Think of it this way. If you tried to explain the joys of sex to a seven-year-old boy, he would think that you were crazy. Chocolate, yes; sex, no. He wants to avoid girls. He doesn't like them at all. In other words, the category is beyond his comprehension. Likewise, Jesus said that heaven is better than anything we can presently imagine."

The Bible says, "No eye has seen, no ear has heard, no mind has conceived what God has prepared for those who love him" (1 Corinthians 2:9). I'm sure of one thing, it won't be a matter of playing or listening to harps forever and ever.

Earlier in this book, I said that the Lord's Prayer is all about the kingdom of God. This kingdom or rule of God is called heaven.

Jesus often referred to the kingdom of God in terms of a banquet. In his parables he often said, "The kingdom of God is like a great banquet ..." Heaven is a party, a happy family party with lots of joy and relationships.

There are many things we don't know about heaven — where it is, what it looks like, etc. — but there are some things we do know about it. It is primarily a matter of a relationship with God through Jesus Christ as the Gospel of John says, "He who believes *has* eternal life" (John 5:24 and 6:47). In theology, that is called realized eschatology. In practical terms that is called present tense religion. Heaven begins *now* when we have a relationship with God through faith in Christ. Eternal life is perfected after death, but it begins in life — *now*. To pray "Our Father in heaven" means that we have a preview of the kingdom right now through Jesus Christ. Heaven means having a relationship with God. Hell is the absence of that relationship. Heaven begins in the here and now and is brought to its completion in life after death. As you come to Holy Communion, you are touched by the heavenly Father with a foretaste of heaven, the heavenly banquet, God's party.

Secular humanism is sweeping across the world. There is no touch of eternity in secular humanism. An immediate gratification syndrome among young and old is evidence of the deep spiritual disease of people today. There is no kingdom content in lop-sided, this-worldly self-centeredness. We need contact with the eternal Father. We need relationship with God through Jesus Christ as the corrective for shortsighted secular humanism and uncaring selfishness. When we point to the heavenly Father in the Lord's Prayer, we find that corrective. We also discover that we are part of the family of God. We pray, "*Our* Father."

Some years ago, when my wife and I traveled in Europe on the way to the Holy Land, we stopped to see the Passion Play in Oberammergau, Germany. The Sunday morning before we saw the play, we attended worship at a small Lutheran church about a block from the theater. The pastor was German. The service and sermon were given in both German and English. It was quite a broadening experience to hear the words of the liturgy in German translated into our native English. When it came time for the Lord's Prayer, the pastor turned to the worshipers and said, "Now I am going to ask you to pray the Lord's Prayer in your native tongue, whatever it may be." One of the great thrills of our trip was to feel the touch of eternity in the here and now and the great fellowship of God's family as we prayed in the languages of the world, "Our Father in heaven...." God's children, who speak all the languages of the world, are one family as they believe in the one true God, our heavenly Father, through Jesus Christ who brings us a touch of eternity in the here and now.

We are called by our heavenly Father to prepare one another for eternity — not just helping people to prepare to die, but helping one another to prepare to live more meaningful lives by adding the touch of eternity as a corrective for the materialism and secular humanism of today. We need an eternal dimension today. We need the kingdom of God! That kingdom comes as we sincerely pray, "Our Father in heaven."

As we pray the Lord's Prayer, we are in touch with our heavenly Father who is always waiting for us to come home. Our home is the kingdom of God. Our heavenly *Abba* is waiting.

The Holy Name Of God

The Lord's Prayer teaches us to pray, "Hallowed be your name." The second commandment says: "You shalt not take the name of the Lord your God in vain." The name of God is of tremendous significance to God's people. The second law of God and the first petition of the Lord's Prayer deal with God's name.

Words often dishonor God's name — words lacking love and compassion, words filled with invective and judgment, words spoken in hot anger against God or people. A friend of mine who works in the construction industry and often hears God's name taken in vain put it this way: "Contrary to popular belief, God's last name is not 'damn.' " Words which take God's name in vain are out of harmony with this prayer petition.

Deeds too. Deeds which dishonor God, deeds of which we can't be proud, deeds which we try to hide from God — they, too, cause our prayer, "hallowed be your name," to be empty of meaning. To pray this petition correctly means that by the power of God we throw unholy words and deeds behind us. Respect, the forgotten virtue of modern times, is the heart of the first petition of the Lord's Prayer. Disrespect is a communicable disease today; it has reached epidemic proportions. Chaos is catching. Often we succumb.

As we consider this petition, we discover our sin and separation from God which comes from giving him so little attention. Giving attention to God means respect. Charles Lamb said, "If Shakespeare walked into this room, we would all rise; but, if Jesus Christ should come in, we would all kneel."

Martin Luther, in one of his expositions of the Lord's Prayer, said about this petition: "I know of no teaching in all the Scriptures that so mightily diminishes and destroys our life as does this petition." He was speaking about diminishing all forms of self-centeredness. We all malign and dishonor God's name by our self-centeredness, by the worship of false gods, by our speech, by our sinful deeds, and by our disrespect for God and for other people.

Helmut Thielicke says: "He who has not yet learned to pray this prayer *de profundus*, out of the depths of repentance, has not really prayed it at all." We have taken the name of God in vain. We have dishonored God's name by idolatry, by wrong words, sinful actions, and by disrespect.

Dietrich Bonhoeffer observed that to believe in God and properly pray the Lord's Prayer means to recognize that God is different from everything else, not just better than everything, for that would imply that he is the best in his class. In fact, nothing is on the same level with God. Everything is below God. That is why we pray, "Hallowed be your name."

To hallow God's name literally means to let God be God, and to treat God as the holy One. Love of everything else, even very good and wholesome family members and precious things, is below God. Respect is restored to everything else only when we respect God who is above everything else. God's name is above every name. How we use God's name indicates what we think of God.

There is a story told about an Army chaplain and a general who were walking along a street one day when they spotted a soldier who was obviously drunk. His uniform was wrinkled; his shirt was pulled out of his pants and his hat was crooked. "Excuse me," said the general to the chaplain. The officer then proceeded to walk up to the soldier and with strength from the anger he was feeling, lifted him high up against a wall and said, "Who do you think you are to dishonor the name of your country like this? You represent the United States of America. Now get your self back to camp and get cleaned up."

The Army chaplain who told the story said, "That's how it is with God." Someone should remind us forcefully that our conduct is representative. We are called to represent God. We often misrepresent him. God is holy. His name is holy. We are called to represent God's name in our words and deeds.

To have faith means to revere God's name. Faith also means that we stake our life on the belief that God knows us by name. God never demands anything without first giving a gift. Before God says, "You shall not take my name in vain," he says, "I know you by name, you are mine."

God is holy. His name is holy. What we say and do indicates what we think of God. But there is something else behind God's insistence that we keep his name holy. God makes our names holy before he demands that we keep his name holy.

A little boy once got a little mixed up when he was praying the Lord's Prayer. He prayed: "Our Father in heaven, how do you know my name?"

"How do you know my name?" the boy asked. How indeed? There are so many people on earth that it is inconceivable God should know them all personally and intimately, but the Bible says that God knows each of us by name. Jesus said, "... even the very hairs of your head are all numbered" (Matthew 10:30). In addition, every one of us has sinned and hurt the Father, the result of which is estrangement. In human affairs, hurt and estrangement are accompanied by name-calling. God overcomes the estrangement from him through Jesus Christ and calls us by name.

Saint Augustine observed that our heavenly Father loves each of us as if there were only one of us. Think of it — all the love of God focused upon each one of us as if God had only one child to love instead of millions upon millions. Before God says, "Keep my name holy," he says, "you, my child. You are made in my image. Therefore, you are holy and you have a holy name." God knows each of his children by name.

To be known by name means to be known individually. A pastor made a home call on a large family and asked, "How many children do you have, Mrs. Jones?" "Well, there's Billy, Joe, Carol and ..." she started. "I just want their number, not their names," the discourteous pastor snapped. "They have names, not numbers," the mother replied. That is how it is with God.

The Lord is not like his sinful children who tend to herd people into categories. He knows no one by labels like Chinese, Jew, or Black. God knows his people by name. "I know my own and my own know me," Jesus once said. Since you are known by name as a person, you are invited to reflect that kind of love and reverence for God and his name.

A visitor to Copenhagen, Denmark, told of visiting the great cathedral there and viewing the famous statues by the gifted sculptor, Thorwaldsen. The guide took the visitor and his party through the cathedral and showed them the six disciples on the north wall and the six disciples on the south wall. Then he led them to the high altar to see the greatest statue of all, that of Jesus the Christ. The visitors were impressed but could not see his face. The guide, with a tone of deep respect and reverence said, "The statue has been designed in a very special way. If you want to see the face of Christ, you must kneel at the feet of Christ." When the visitors knelt and looked up from that position of deep respect, they saw the holiness of God reflected in the face of Jesus.

That is what it is like to pray these words, "Our Father in heaven, hallowed be your name."

Questions And Ideas
For Your Consideration And Discussion

1. Why do people abuse God's name?

2. Bible scholars tell us that God's proper name in Hebrew was "Yahweh" which means "I am who I am." What does that mean? In respect for that name, and fear of misusing that name, the Jews did not speak that name at all. They wrote it but did not use it in speaking of God. Since the vowels in the Hebrew language were added later, the written word looked like this: "YHWH."

    Compare that kind of respect with the the way God's name is abused in language today.

3. Count the number of times you hear the name of God taken in vain this next week. Record the number here. _____

Chapter 3

Your Kingdom Come

This, then is how you should pray: Our Father in heaven, hallowed be your name, your kingdom come, your will be done on earth as it is in heaven.
— Matthew 6:9-10

* * *

In our study of the Lord's Prayer, we began by looking at *Abba*, our Father. Next we looked at God's name. We continue the study of the Lord's Prayer by focusing on the kingdom of God.

Martin Luther said, "God's kingdom comes indeed without our praying for it. But we ask in this prayer that it may come also to us." Let's look at three questions to get at the meaning of this petition. What? When? How?

What?

What is God's kingdom? The kingdom means that God is the center of our lives — not self, not spouse, not children, not job, not money — but God! Jesus said, "Seek first the kingdom of God" (Matthew 6:33). The kingdom is first, not second or third, but first! God's kingdom means that God reigns over us for our own good. Accepting the rule of God for our lives is the one thing needful and the hardest of all.

The entire Bible can be outlined under the theme of the kingdom of God. Chapters one and two of Genesis tell us that God created everything to be under his reign. Chapter three shows Adam and Eve rebelling against God's reign. In chapter four of Genesis through the end of the book of Revelation, God seeks to re-establish his reign over us for our own good, while respecting our freedom to say "No" to him.

What is the kingdom of God? *God's kingdom is his reign over us for our own good.* Like a parent who tells his young son or daughter not to put his hand in the fire or run out into the traffic on the highway, God acts in love through his lordship. Like a parent welcoming home a rebellious child, God embraces us with mercy and grace when we return to the wonders of his lordship.

When?

When does the kingdom come? The three time zones for the kingdom of God are past, future, and present!

The kingdom *has* come. That is past tense. It was ushered in when Jesus came to earth. Jesus said, "The kingdom of God is near" (Mark 1:15).

The kingdom *will* come. That is future tense. Repeatedly Jesus warned his followers to get ready for the ultimate judgment day when the kingdom will come with fullness.

The kingdom *comes now.* That's present tense. We live between the first (past) and the second (future) coming of Christ. We live between the lightning and the thunder. In the here and now in Word and sacraments, the kingdom of God comes to us in the present.

Let's back up and look again in greater detail at the three time zones for the kingdom of God.

The kingdom of God has come. About 2,000 years ago, God became a man in Jesus Christ and brought the kingdom of God with him. He announced the great truths of the kingdom over and over again, "The kingdom of God is like a father who gave his prodigal son enough freedom to leave home"; "The kingdom of God is like a man who sold everything he had to buy the pearls of great price"; "The kingdom of God is like a man who built bigger and bigger barns, became rich, only to hear the cry against him, 'You fool, tonight your soul shall be required of you.' " When Jesus came, the kingdom came.

The kingdom is also coming in the future. Jesus promised that at the end of the world the kingdom would be brought to perfection. The fulfillment of our hope in Christ is something for which we wait. We wait in faith, seeing only "reflections in a glass darkly" as Saint Paul so eloquently states in 1 Corinthians 13. "Then (i.e., in the future), we shall see face-to-face." God's kingdom is a thing of the future as well as of the past. It is also a present reality.

The kingdom of God is here, now. It not only has come; it not only will come; it comes now. The urgency of Paul's words about "the acceptable time" indicates that he was talking about the kingdom as present reality. "Behold now is the day of salvation," he says (2 Corinthians 6:2). Jesus puts it this way: "Very truly, I tell you, whoever believes has eternal life" (John 6:47, NRSV). In theology that is called "realized eschatology." In plain words it means that eternal life begins in the here and now.

When we pray, "Your kingdom come," we are praying not only that one day God's promise of the full deliverance from sin, death, evil, and all suffering will come, and that we are in harmony with that plan for the future through faith and hope; not only that, but also that the kingdom of God comes to our hearts now. This day and every day is a day of salvation for anyone who will believe. This day and every day is a day to spread the gospel. This is a kingdom of God day.

Now that we have looked at the first question about the kingdom of God (*What?*), and the second question (*When?*), let us turn to the third question: *How?*

How?

The third basic question about the kingdom of God is how it comes. Martin Luther wrote, "The kingdom of God comes without our prayer; but we pray in this petition that it may come unto us also." He was advocating present tense praying. He was urging us to witness to others about the one true God. He wanted us to understand that the kingdom of God comes *to us* in order to go *through us* to others. This is a present-tense personal petition. We pray that the kingdom of God might present touch us and through us, touch others.

We pray for this kingdom coming now, to come to us and go through us. The kingdom of God is wherever Jesus Christ is, where he is known and loved. Jesus is everywhere, but he is not everywhere known and loved. In some places Christ is only a swear word. In some people's lives, Jesus is unknown as the living Lord of life. How does the kingdom of God come today? Through people who love God and say so. Through people who have faith in Christ and share that faith.

A shoemaker in Scotland became a Christian late in life. He said to one of his regular customers, "I must tell you about what God has done for me so that maybe you, too, will want to become a Christian."

"Oh, I am a Christian," said the customer.

"If that is so," replied the shoemaker, "why haven't you mentioned it over the twenty years I've known you?"

"It never occurred to me," replied the customer.

How does the kingdom come to people today? Through people who love God and don't neglect to show it. It also comes through people who are sent to us by God at critical times.

A friend recently told me the story of how he came back from a major depression that caused him to contemplate suicide. He put it this way:

> *A few years back, I found myself in the greatest trial of my life, the most devastating experience I had ever encountered. I was totally shattered. All my hopes and dreams, all that I had lived for and believed in were suddenly swept away. My life had ended. I was a complete failure. I felt that I had nothing left to live for. God had forsaken me and I was left all alone in my sorrow and deep despair. I contemplated suicide.*
>
> *I found no comfort in the church. There was no wise counsel to console me, no faith to lift me up, and my knowledge of Scripture completely failed me. What had once been a living word was now a dead letter. I was too angry at God to pray. The condition continued for many months.*

> Then one day a seemingly insignificant encounter with a child changed my life. I was coming home from work and as I entered my apartment complex, a little boy three or four years old ran up in front of me. He stretched out his little arms, blocking the sidewalk so that I could not pass. Then he said something that I did not understand. So I dropped to one knee in front of him and asked, "What did you say, son?"
> "Mister, do you wike to hug wittle kids?"
> "Sure, son," I replied. "Do you need a hug?"
> "Uh huh."
> I gave him a big hug and he hugged me in return. Then I continued on to my apartment, but as I opened the door some strange things began to happen to me. There were lights turning on inside my head. Everything I looked at became lighter and brighter. A flow of tremendous love engulfed me with peace and joy.
>
> Suddenly, I realized that I was being lifted up out of my cloud of depression and sorrow. I was placed into a cloud of love, all in an instant. The cloud of depression was still there, but it was under me, under my feet. I could still see it, but it could no longer hold me within its grasp. I was able to see and understand my anger, my self-pity, my crushed ego and my guilt. I saw all the ingredients that work together to create such an oppressive state. In my darkest hour, when nothing else could help, love came to me uninvited. Love lifted me.

A little child was a transparent witness for the kingdom of God for my friend. Jesus appeared to him in the form of a child who needed a hug. He returned from despair to a productive life through the love of Jesus expressed by that child. God sends people to us to speak the right word at the right time to turn us back to him. If we only have ears to hear, we can make the journey of faith renewal through these messengers of God.

Jesus never forced anyone to believe. He just invited people to come back to God. Jesus never pushed anyone into the kingdom. He just attracted people with his great love. Jesus was perfect; we are not, but the kingdom comes to people through imperfect, sinful people like us. We should not pray, "Your kingdom come," unless we intend to bear witness to our faith in Christ and his kingdom. The kingdom comes through common people like us. To pray, "Your kingdom come," and then act as if you did not believe your own words or that you don't care much about other people, is hypocrisy. When we pray, "Your kingdom come," we are pledging ourselves to work for its actualization in the lives of people today.

Of course, we don't usher in the kingdom. That is God's business, but he gives his children the dignity to be witnesses for his kingdom of love. Our method of reaching out to others for the sake of the kingdom must be like that of Jesus. He shared the good news of the kingdom with love and humility. We must do the same as we humbly pray, "Your kingdom come."

Questions And Ideas
For Your Consideration And Discussion

1. Describe the kingdom of God in your own words.

2. What difference does it make that the kingdom of God has come, will come, and does come?

3. How can we be better witnesses for God and his kingdom?

Chapter 4

Your Will Be Done On Earth As It Is In Heaven

This then is how you should pray ... Your will be done on earth as it is in heaven. — Matthew 6:10

* * *

What are we praying in this petition? What does "Your will be done on earth as it is in heaven" mean? Luther answered that question like this: "The good and gracious will of God is done indeed without our prayer; but we pray in this petition that it may be done among us also."

What Is And What Isn't God's Will?

There is more confusion about the will of God than about any other topic. Let's look first at what is not the will of God. For example, when there is a hurricane, a tornado, or a flood, what does the insurance company call it? They call it "an act of God." How confusing! How distorted! How twisted our minds have become in this fallen state that we should attribute disasters to God. At funerals, people often say, "It was the will of God that he (she) died." Irreparable damage can be caused by attributing suffering and death to God's will.

John Randolf puts it this way:

> *The will of God is on the side of light and healing and goodness. God is on our side; not against us.*
>
> *I think we are going to have to find other explanations for many of the things we have too easily identified*

> as the will of God. There are times when we simply
> have to say, "Call it evil, call it human irresponsibility,
> call it natural phenomenon we don't yet understand,
> but don't call it the will of God."²

Before we call something the will of God, we should check to make sure that it is consistent with what Jesus taught us about God.

Dr. Leslie Weatherhead has written a helpful book called *The Will of God* in which he attacks the many illusions we have about God's will. Among other helpful things he says, "Surely we cannot identify as the will of God something for which a man would be locked up in jail, or put in a criminal lunatic asylum."

In Matthew 18:14 we read: "It is not the will of my Father who is in heaven, that any of these little ones should perish." Jesus did not inflict disease on anyone. On the contrary, he healed countless numbers of sick people. God is on the side of healing, not hurting; life, not death. The will of God is for health and wholeness.

Like a father who wills only good for his recalcitrant son or daughter, nevertheless God respects the son's or daughter's freedom to turn away from him, as well as to make good decisions. God does not force good on his children. God does not take away freedom, even when we misuse or abuse that freedom. The abuse of freedom causes much of the trouble we have in life. Some tragedies remain unexplained, but many come from the misuse of freedom by God's children.

Fivefold Test

There are still many mysteries about God's will for which we will get answers when we see him face-to-face, but as you pray this petition about God's will, you might want to consider this five-fold test for determining what the will of God is for you personally:

1. Jesus revealed God in the Scriptures. Is what you are seeking contrary to or in agreement with God's Word?
2. Jesus revealed God to be loving. Is what you seek in prayer reflective of a loving God?
3. Jesus revealed God to be holy. Is the object of your prayer reflective of a holy God?

4. Jesus revealed God to be just. Is your petition before God reflective of a God who is just?
5. Jesus revealed a God who suffers with his people. Are you praying in harmony with God who suffers with his people?

As you come away from prayer and consider your actions, ask yourself, "Am I really seeking to do the will of God? If so, how shall I do it?" The answer is that we are called to do the will of God joyfully and willingly, like the angels in heaven do it. "Your will be done on earth as it is done in heaven," we pray.

Do the angels do the will of God sadly? Of course not. Neither should we! Do the angels grumble at the will of God? No. Neither should we! Aren't the angels gleeful and joyful in doing the will of God? Yes. So we, too, should pray to do the will of God as in heaven!

To pray, "Your will be done," means to seek to do as much as we know of the will of God joyfully and willingly! We pray in this petition that our will be adapted to God's will, not reluctantly through clenched teeth, but out of the knowledge that God wants only good for us.

To pray, "Your will be done," means to recognize that God the Father is for us, not against us. Thus we unravel the tangled knot of resistance to God's will in our minds. Resistance to God is not only the problem of Adam and Eve. It is our problem as well.

To pray this prayer means that we recognize the need to overcome the human tendency to center our lives in ourselves. Not until this balance is redressed — not until the world is no longer seen as revolving around each individual ego, which is the sun, and everybody else just satellites — will any political or social or economic system work for the full benefit of mankind, instead of for a powerful few. The purpose of the Christian religion is to make us God-centered rather than man-centered; thus we see the importance attached to these words, "Your will be done."

Reinhold Niebuhr once observed: "If the self-centered is shattered by a genuine awareness of its situation, there is the power of a new life in the experience." That awareness is implicit in these words, "Your will be done." That awareness leads to witness to others about the kingdom of God.

To pray this petition means we open ourselves to be instruments of God to usher his kingdom into the hearts of others.

We dare not just rattle these words off like the grocery list. "Your will be done on earth as it is in heaven" is the center of our faith and the heart of our problem. Self-centeredness, or the illusion of our individuality, is our biggest problem. Bluntly stated, we have a natural propensity towards asking God, or sometimes telling God, to do our will instead of trying to tune into his will. The object of prayer is not that God's will might be changed, but that God's will might be known and done by us.

The AA Prayer May Be Helpful

The prayer of Alcoholics Anonymous (AA) may be helpful in this respect:

> *Lord, give me the courage to change the things I can change, the serenity to accept the things I cannot change, and the wisdom to know the difference.*

Instead of accepting those things we cannot change, we often fight these things. It's like beating our heads against a brick wall to try to change those things which cannot be changed.

Instead of accepting those things we cannot change, we sometimes resent them. We try to grin and bear some trouble or disappointment, but inside we are angry. Resentment is internalized anger. Resentment is a major flaw in most of our lives. It kills our physical and spiritual health.

Instead of accepting those things we cannot change, sometimes we try to resign ourselves to them. Acceptance and resignation are two different things. Acceptance is positive and healthy. Resignation is negative and non-productive. We often hear phrases like "He is resigned to his lot," the meaning of which is that a person has forced himself by an act of the will to accept a most difficult fact of life. Sometimes "Your will be done" is prayed in that mood. "Well, Lord, if you won't heal my mother or change my husband or make my son be more attentive, then your will be done." These words said through clenched teeth are counter-productive. That kind of a doom and gloom attitude is not at all what our Lord had in mind in teaching us this prayer petition.

This petition means acceptance, not resignation! Acceptance happens as we fall to our knees and open ourselves to God, turning from self to God as the center of our lives. To center one's life in God means accepting those things one cannot change. It also means willing obedience.

Jesus once said, "My food is to do the will of my father." He was driven to fulfill the spiritual hunger of man through the will of the Father like a natural man is driven to fulfill physical hunger by seeking food. In other words, the will of God was not just something Jesus accepted because it couldn't be changed, but something he anticipated and expected and desired and struggled to know. It was his food — his life supply.

To do the will of the Father on earth as it is in heaven means to embrace the ways of God. That's how the angels do it — joyfully and willingly embracing God's will.

Yes, but even when we seek to do the will of God joyfully and willingly, sometimes things go wrong and bad things happen to us. This petition, "Your will be done," raises a serious question: *Where is God when bad things happen to us?*

The answer to that question is that God always identifies with the sufferer. Jesus is the Suffering Servant. When you suffer, he suffers with you. He willfully identifies with all your suffering. When you realize this astounding truth, you can pray joyfully and willingly, "Your will be done on earth as it is in heaven."

Dr. Helmut Thielicke, in his book on the Lord's Prayer, offers this comforting thought: "Everything that happens to you whether good or bad, must pass muster before your Father's heart."[3]

We sing about the God who cares in one of our famous hymns, "Jesus Calls Us O'er The Tumult." Jesus doesn't cause the tumult. He is in the tumult *with us*. He suffers through it *with us*. He stands *with us*. And he calls us over the noisy clatter of our own willfulness or the noisy roar of the disaster: "Follow me, I will get you through the tumult."

The Lord's Prayer is centered in the glory of our *Abba*. True prayer always is. Prayer is basically a matter of opening oneself to God and not trying to manipulate God or trying to get God to do our bidding. Opening the door to Jesus, who stands knocking, gives glory to God and hallows his name. One of the highest expressions of being centered in God and not in ourselves is mysteriously hidden in this prayer petition: "Your will be done on earth as it is in heaven...."

Questions And Ideas
For Your Consideration And Discussion

1. Do you agree or disagree with the fivefold test of the will of God?

2. Do you agree with the statement, "God works through all things that happen to us, but does not cause all things that happen to us"?

Chapter 5

Give Us Tomorrow's Bread Today

> *This, then is how you should pray: Our Father in heaven, hallowed be your name, your kingdom come, your will be done on earth as it is in heaven. Give us this day our daily bread.*   — Matthew 6:9-11

* * *

In 1988 while on sabbatical leave studying in Canterbury, England, I was privileged to hear Bishop John V. Taylor, an Anglican theologian, author and teacher, give a lecture on the Lord's Prayer and the kingdom of God. "The whole of the Lord's Prayer is about the kingdom of God," he said, "not just the petition, 'Your kingdom come.' " The petition before us, "Give us today our daily bread" (Matthew 6:11), is about the kingdom of God.

Among the most important things which Bishop Taylor pointed out is the possibility that in the Lord's Prayer "Give us this day our daily bread" may mean far more than thanksgiving for three square meals a day. "Alternatively," he said, "Jesus' original meaning, coming from the Aramaic word *machar*,[4] may have meant, 'Give us tomorrow's bread today,' that is 'Give us the bread of the kingdom now.' "

Tomorrow's bread is the food of the kingdom of God. The kingdom is not fully here, but in the person of Jesus, a breakthrough came, a preview was seen. The kingdom, the power, and the glory of God break through wherever Jesus is. While the fullness of the kingdom of God will not come until the end of time, in Jesus we experience the end of time now in "tomorrow's bread."

Tomorrow's bread is the food necessary to strengthen us for being kingdom people. Tomorrow's bread is spiritual food for the spiritual journey of life. Since the Lord's Prayer is about the kingdom, this alternative translation is particularly helpful for disciples who are called to witness to people about the kingdom of God. We feel unworthy to be called kingdom witnesses. "We are needy sinners. We can't do that," we protest. "We are too weak." Exactly. That's why we need tomorrow's bread. Tomorrow's bread is nourishment and strength from God for this mission impossible.

Where do we find this spiritual food? Where do we get this "manna" from heaven for the journey in the wilderness? What form does this bread from tomorrow for today come? Consider three sources of tomorrow's kingdom bread: 1) prayer, 2) God's Word, and 3) the Sacrament.

Prayer

Tomorrow's bread comes in prayer. Spiritual food is given as disciples spend time with God, listening, talking, and sharing with *Abba*. *Abba* is the Aramaic word which Jesus used in prayer. It means Daddy. The personal intimacy of a son or daughter talking to his or her father about joys and concerns and listening for guidance is the heart of the Lord's Prayer. The Lord's Prayer is also the family prayer. First, it is Jesus' prayer. Second, it is the prayer of the family of God.

Henri Nouwen, the Roman Catholic spiritual writer, describes prayer that feeds the souls of the people of God on mission for God as opening our hands to God.

> *To pray means to open your hands before God. It means slowly relaxing the tension, which squeezes your hands together, and accepting your existence with an increasing readiness, not as a possession to defend, but as a gift to receive. Above all, therefore, prayer is a way of life which allows you to find a stillness in the midst of the world where you open your hands to God's promises, and find hope for yourself, your neighbor, and your world.*[5]

Consider the word "bread." We easily take bread for granted. We need to think about what bread means. It is in the breaking of bread together that some of the basic realities of life are experienced. Eating together has always been a symbol of friendship and fellowship between persons. "Let us break bread together" since ancient times has been an invitation to come close and share, to open yourself to the basic "stuff" of meaningful relationships. Prayer can give us the sustenance for the life we need as Christians.

Consider the fact that this is not just a personal prayer to my Father for my bread, but a family prayer for *our* Father to give *us* tomorrow's bread. In other words, those who are insensitive to the needs of others do not properly pray the prayer. To pray this prayer properly, the people in the "Me Generation" will have to reverse the "me first" attitude. The biblical corrective for too much "me" is to concentrate on God, other people, and community. Prayer can sustain us to do just that.

Consider the word "today" in this petition. To pray in the present tense is to be fed with the bread of life, to be nourished by God today, to be strengthened for today's life's journey. To open your hands to God means for us to receive tomorrow's bread *today.*

The Old Testament story of the Exodus and the gift of bread from heaven for the wandering people of God reminds us of the importance of thanking God on a daily basis and taking each day as it comes. The people of God were wandering through the wilderness and muttering that perhaps they should have stayed in Egypt and in bondage, for as they said: "At least we had food when we were slaves." Then Moses came forth with a great promise from Yahweh. "There will be food," he said, "meat in the evening and manna fresh each morning." The prophet-patriarch warned the wandering Hebrews that the danger connected with the promise was that the bread from heaven, the manna (a white substance which exudes from one of the plants in the desert) must be consumed each day and that the new day would have food enough for them.

The Lord brought the people quail each evening and bread each morning. The people received the bread from heaven each morning as promised, but they were afraid that they might be forgotten one day. Perhaps it would rain and God wouldn't deliver the promised food. Perhaps God would be preoccupied and forget them one day. Maybe they would sin and the angry Yahweh would hold back on his promise. So they tried to store up their manna from one day to the next — the very thing they were warned not to do.

People are strange, aren't they? In their freedom, they often choose the very things God has forbidden for their own good. The command to gather the manna fresh each morning wasn't an arbitrary and dictatorial order, but a warning from the concerned Father to receive blessings daily.

People get mixed up, don't they? An eight-year-old was asked to describe the Exodus to his Sunday school class. He said, "That's when Moses led the Hebrew slaves to the Red Sea, where they made unleavened bread, which is bread made without any ingredients (yeast). Moses went up to Mount Cyanide (Sinai) to get the Ten Commandments. He died before he ever reached Canada (Cana)."

Those were minor mistakes in language. Sometimes the mistakes people make are in the area of substance.

One of the major mistakes about the Exodus is to think that you can store up God's manna for the future. The manna, which the Hebrews tried to preserve, rotted. It could not be kept for more than a day at a time. It had to be gathered fresh each day. The word "daily" takes on a new significance in the light of this great story from the Exodus of the Hebrews.

Jesus put a strong emphasis on relying on God in prayer on a daily basis. He knew human nature better than anyone who has ever lived. He knew that even people who were very dedicated believers could fall away; that even those who worked for the kingdom could easily fade from their dedication through temptations. Therefore, Jesus called for feeding through daily prayer. He also called for renewal through the Word and the Sacrament.

The Word And The Sacrament

Prayer is a place of nourishment. So is the Word of God. The preaching of the Word is not a lecture on a religious topic by a professional with a degree in theology. Preaching is God's saving Word as Saint Paul says:

> *Every one who calls upon the name of the Lord will be saved. But how are men to call upon him in whom they have not believed? And how are they to believe in him of whom they have never heard? And how are they to hear without a preacher? And how can men preach unless they are sent? As it is written, "How beautiful are the feet of those who preach good news!" But they have not all heeded the gospel; for Isaiah says, "Lord, who has believed what he has heard from us?" So faith comes from what is heard, and what is heard comes by the preaching of Christ.* — Romans 10:13-17, RSV

The preaching of the Word nourishes our souls. So does the study of God's Word. In both private study of God's Word and in group study, God nourishes our souls with tomorrow's bread today.

Holy Communion is also "tomorrow's bread today." As we come to Holy Communion, we receive much more than bread and wine. We receive Christ *in, through,* or *under* the elements of bread and wine. We receive tomorrow's bread today. We receive spiritual nourishment for our souls.

The parable of the waiting father (Luke 15:1-32) is a case in point. The younger son had blown his inheritance on wine, women, and song. His inheritance gone, his friends having deserted him, he "came to himself" and started home with the slight hope that maybe his father would allow him to be a servant. Instead, the waiting father rejoiced at his return and restored him to full family status as a son. He threw a banquet for his returning son for "he was dead and is now alive; he was lost, but now is found." When the younger son came home from the far-off country, there was a sign of the kingdom in the banqueting.

The Lord's Supper is that kind of banqueting celebration of the family of God, a breaking in of the good news that the Father's arms are always open to his children. We see through the shadows of reality and find the heart of God in the Lord's Supper. We receive tomorrow's bread today in the kingdom banquet for sinners who have come home to God.

Thus the petition, "Give us tomorrow's bread today," is literally answered when we hear and believe the Word of God saying, "The Body and Blood of Christ, given and shed for you."

Questions And Ideas
For Your Consideration And Discussion

1. How does the translation of daily bread as "tomorrow's bread today" change the way you think about and pray the Lord's Prayer?

2. Does this translation make a difference in the way you live?

Chapter 6

Forgive Us

This then is how you should pray ... "Forgive us our debts, as we also have forgiven our debtors ... For if you forgive men when they sin against you, your heavenly Father will also forgive you." — Matthew 6:9-14

* * *

Some years ago I was talking about handling problems to a friend who is a recovering alcoholic. I asked him a question: "What is the difference between the way you are now and the way you were when you were drinking?" "I still have problems," he said, "but I now realize that I have to stop trying to change everybody else and that the real change has to come inside me, not others. I have learned the hard way that everything depends on my attitude. It's not a matter of what happens in life and not a matter of how other people act. Success in life depends on my attitude." He went on to explain how he previously blamed other people for his troubles and how he often felt sorry for himself because of the troubles which came his way. "I have come to a new understanding of myself and a new dependence on God each day," he said. Then he put it all together in one easy to remember sentence: "The proper attitude toward God is gratitude for grace and the proper attitude toward people is forgiveness."

That's what Christ was driving at in the petition of the Lord's Prayer about forgiveness. The attitude of forgiveness toward others is based on the attitude of gratitude toward God for his forgiveness. This petition focuses our attention on our attitude toward God and other people.

Forgive Us ... As We Forgive

The apparent problem in this petition is what to call our sins. Are they trespasses? Wrongs? Or debts? Different Christians use different words in this petition. Presbyterians use "debts" in their prayers. Roman Catholics generally pray, "Forgive us our trespasses." Lutherans generally pray, "Forgive us our sins as we forgive those who sin against us." The words are only the apparent problem. You can use any of these words. The real problem is the last part of the petition, "... as we forgive those who sin against us." The real problem is how to adjust our attitude about God's gracious forgiveness, so that we treat other people as God treats us.

One woman told me that every Sunday as she prayed the Lord's Prayer in church, this phrase got stuck in her throat. She found that she frequently coughed when she started to say, "as we forgive." "What if God treated us exactly as we treat our neighbors?" she said. "None of us would have any hope at all." The petition does not mean that God is going to treat us exactly as we have treated others, but it certainly does mean that when God forgives us, he expects us to reflect his forgiveness in our human relationships. He expects us to throw their lives behind our prayers. When we try to hoard God's grace and fail to give it away, we lose it. When we try to keep forgiveness to ourselves, it slips away.

Jesus told the parable of the unforgiving servant in Matthew 18:21-35. This is a parable about the need to be an agent of God's forgiveness, not just a recipient of forgiveness. He told the story specifically because Peter asked about how many times we should forgive our brothers. "As many as seven times?" Peter asked. Jesus answered, "No, not seven times, but seventy times seven," i.e., without limit. Then Jesus told the story of a king to whom a servant was indebted for millions of dollars. The servant did not have enough money even to begin to pay his debt, so his master ordered him to be sold as a slave along with his wife and children. The man fell on his knees and pleaded with his master. The master was moved, so by grace he forgave him the debt.

The servant went out and met his fellow servant who owed him a few dollars. He grabbed him and started choking him. "Pay me," he shouted. Then the fellow servant fell down and begged him, "Be patient with me and I will pay you back," using the same plea that the man had used with his master. But he would not listen and had his fellow servant thrown into jail. When the master found out, he called the man before him and said, "You worthless slave! I forgave you the whole amount you owed me because you asked me to do it. You should have had mercy on your fellow servant, just as I had mercy on you." "That," said Jesus, "is how my Father in heaven will treat you if you do not forgive your brother, every one of you, from your heart."

Three basic things about forgiveness are noted in this parable. The three ingredients in forgiveness are *justice*, *mercy*, and *grace*. Justice means getting what you deserve. Mercy means not getting what you deserve. Grace means getting what you do not deserve.

First, forgiveness is not a substitute for justice. When there is no genuine repentance or no gratitude for forgiveness, justice must be done. The servant who was not grateful for the grace of his master was punished severely. What a man sows, he reaps. The unforgiving servant eventually got what he deserved.

Second, mercy permeates the parable. Initially, the servant did not get what he deserved. The master was merciful toward him when he had an unmanageable debt. He deserved prison. He got forgiveness.

Third, the master went beyond mercy all the way to grace. The servant got what he did not deserve — a clean slate, the chance to start life again, debt free. Grace is God's free gift to undeserving servants. Our sins our wiped away by God's grace in Jesus Christ. The recipient of grace appeared to be grateful. Apparently, he said, "Thank you," but we discover that he was not really grateful because he did not pass on to others what he had received.

Notice that God acts first with forgiveness. Only then does he expect us to reflect his mercy. He is not saying that his grace is conditional and that he will only be good and merciful to us if we are good and merciful to others. *God is merciful and gracious.* But if we don't share God's mercy and grace, we lose it.

Notice, too, that the amount owed the master far exceeds the debt between the servants. That's how it is with God. The debt we owe him far exceeds any debt that any person owes us. The parable of the unforgiving servant is a good point of departure in considering Jesus' words, "Forgive us ... as we forgive." It points out that an unforgiving spirit slams the door in God's face.

Notice in the parable that there is an inexorable law of stagnation described in the story. If you don't use the forgiveness you receive, you lose that forgiveness. What comes to you as mercy and grace must pass through you to others. That is why Jesus taught us to pray, "Forgive us ... as we forgive others."

The natural tendency of humans is to be good to those who are good to us and to try to get even with those who hurt us. This orientation toward retaliation is the heart of the matter. It might be argued with no small amount of evidence that the heart and center of Jesus' teaching is love for one's enemies, i.e. forgiveness instead of retaliation for those who hurt us. Reciprocity is the same whether it is a Corsican blood feud, a western "hero" avenging his father's death by taking the law into his own hands, a wife refusing sex to punish her husband, or a husband who tries to "get even" by being very quiet so that his wife will suddenly realize how she has hurt him. Kids "get even" with one another. Employees and employers pay one another back. Former friends even up the debt. Parents and children are constantly involved in playing the self-defeating game of reciprocity.

A physicist friend once told me about one of the reasons he did not become a pastor. He is related indirectly to the great patriarch of Lutheranism in America, Henry Muhlenberg. "My father was a pastor in Pennsylvania," he said. He then went on to explain that when he was young, many people had told him he should go into the ministry, but he had decided to get a Ph.D. in physics instead and he was glad that he did. "I could never put up with all the terrible things my father had to endure," he said. "In one of his congregations the treasurer often refused to pay him his salary check, because he did not like the sermon that week. If I were in the ministry and that happened to me, I'd excommunicate him!" We had a good laugh at that one, but that feeling of getting even is no laughing matter.

Jesus said, "Love your enemies, do good to them that hate you, and pray for them which spitefully use you." He pointed out that if we only love those who love us back we are no better than the pagans who do the same. In the Sermon on the Mount (Matthew 5:43-48), Jesus points out that Christians are called to be like God, i.e., willing to forgive even enemies who hurt and mistreat them. This is what our faith is all about. This is what Christian love means. This is why "as we forgive" is so important in this petition.

Without an attitude of forgiveness and a willingness to turn the other cheek, the endless screw of retaliation goes on turning, generating more and more retaliation. The proliferation of sin results when people neglect the meaning of this petition or just say the words of this petition with no intention to put them into action by having a forgiving attitude toward others.

To be willing to forgive those who hurt you means having an attitude like God has toward you. God is willing to forgive you even if you do not repent. If you do not repent, you don't reap the benefits of forgiveness, but that doesn't mean that God doesn't offer forgiveness. Likewise, we have no control over whether those who have offended us repent, but we do have control over whether or not we are willing to forgive. To be sensitive to other people's problems and courteous about their limitations is to act as God acts toward you. It means to have the mind of Christ, to see people the way that Christ sees them. On the cross Jesus said, "Father, forgive them for they know not what they do."

Martin Luther said in *The Small Catechism* that the meaning of this petition is to have a charitable attitude toward those who hurt us. For me, there is no excuse for bad behavior. For you, I should always try to find a charitable way to interpret what you do.

Goethe, the famous German literary figure, once observed, "One only understands what one loves." Jesus loved his enemies. That's why he understood them and had a willingness to forgive them.

Offering forgiveness to our enemies is not a matter of trying harder, but of hearing and seeing and understanding what is really happening inside our enemies. By our own power we cannot offer forgiveness to those who hurt us, but the Holy Spirit can cause us to reflect our attitude of gratitude for what God has done for us in Christ by offering forgiveness to others. This brings us to a consideration of the meaning of forgiveness.

The Meaning Of Being Forgiven — The Right Attitude

Recently, while talking to friends about the frustration of long distance phone calls, my mind ran wild about a possible phone call to heaven about forgiveness. In my imagination the call went something like this: (Dialing G-O-D)

Getting a busy signal, I said out loud, "Is God too busy for me?"

Finally getting through, I got an answering machine. I thought all answering machines went to hell.

An angelic voice said, "If you know you are a sinner, press 1. If you think you are not a sinner, hang up and start again."

I pressed 1. "If you repent," said the recorded voice, "press 2. If you do not repent, hang up and think about it." I pressed 2.

"If you are grateful to God for his forgiveness, press 3." By now I was so frustrated that I slammed down the phone with impatience. "I'm grateful to God," I said, "but I hate recorded messages." Calming down, I tried it again. 1. 2. 3. "Yes," I said out loud, "I am grateful." The angel's recorded voice said, "Then why are you talking through clenched teeth? Now hang up the phone, get in touch with the peace of God which passes all understanding, and start again."

I followed the instruction, prayed for peace, and once again pressed the phone buttons, 1, 2, 3. "That's better," said the recorded message, "now press 4." I did. "Now that you are at peace with God, press 5 if you are willing to forgive all the people who have hurt you or sinned against you. If you are not ready to do this, hang up and get your act together."

Of course, you can't call God on the phone, but prayers about forgiveness do require both an attitude of gratitude toward God and a willingness to pass God's forgiveness on to others.

Before you can be forgiven, you must confess your sin. Before you confess, you must see your sinfulness for what it is. Before forgiveness can be complete, you must be willing to forgive others, even if they don't deserve it, just as God is willing to forgive your sins when you don't deserve it.

You can think of your sins in many ways. Here are three:

Trespassing. We've all seen "No Trespassing" signs. When we pray, "Forgive us our trespasses," we mean that we have gone beyond the bounds that God has set for our lives. God said to Adam, "You can have everything, but this one thing." Like Adam, we seek the forbidden thing. When God says, "Here is a code of morality which will make you happy if you follow it," we say, "That's good, Lord, but we have a new code of morality which allows for premarital and extramarital sexual relationships and living together without being married as long as both people agree." That is trespassing, because God has set boundaries which we are ignoring.

Wrongs. When we pray, "Forgive us our wrongs as we forgive those who have wronged us," we acknowledge what some ignore, namely, that there is a standard which describes right and wrong. Ethical relativism runs rampant today. Of course, many things are relative. What seemed wrong last year may be viewed by the mores of today's society as being right, but two things are absolute — God's love and God's law, the Ten Commandments. These are not the mores of society, nor the invention of human beings, but the eternal laws of God. We do wrong when we act contrary to the love of God, or when we break God's commandments.

Debts. This is the word used in the *NIV* in Matthew 6:14. A debt is something I owe. What do I owe God? *Gratitude for what he has done for me in Christ.* What do we owe one another? *Respect, love, and the offer of forgiveness.* Respect means that I acknowledge your right to be different and don't try to use you or manipulate you for my own ends. Love means that I treat you as God does by acting toward you with your good (not mine) in mind. Forgiveness means offering to make peace, even when I have been deeply hurt. That's why we pray, "Forgive us our debts."

Trespasses, wrongs, and debts are all sins. We have sinned and we have been sinned against. When we reflect on our human condition in the light of Christ and his Church, we find a depth there which was previously unknown. We get to know previously unknown parts of ourselves when we get to know Jesus Christ — evil parts that we had never before admitted and good parts (gifts) we had never before imagined. Contact with Christ means awareness of the repressed parts of our minds which had created cramped and inhibited spirits. Having a relationship with Christ and receiving his grace means awareness of the repressed parts of our souls that had created cramped and self-defeating life patterns. In the context of Christian community, we can confess our sins because we are loved.

An anonymous story about computers may help to drive this point home. A customer approached a representative of the JC Company with a computer problem. "Are you ready to install a new system?" the representative asked.

Customer: "I am not very technical, but I am ready to try."

JC Rep: "The first step is to open your *heart*, ma'am."

Customer: "Yes, I have done that, but there are several programs running right now. Is it okay to install while they are running?"

JC Rep: "What programs are running?"

Customer: "Let me see. I have PASTHURT.NET, LOWESTEEM.EXE, GRUDGE.COM and RESENTMENT.COM running right now."

JC Rep: "LOVE will automatically erase PASTHURT from your current operating system. It may remain in your permanent memory, but it will no longer disrupt other programs. LOVE will override LOWESTEEM with a module of its own called HIGHESTEEM. However, you have to completely turn off GRUDGE and RESENTMENT. Those programs prevent LOVE from being properly installed. Can you turn those off, ma'am?"

Customer: "I don't know how. Can you show me how?"

JC Rep: "My pleasure. Go to your START menu and invoke FORGIVENESS. Do this as many times as necessary until GRUDGE and RESENTMENT have been completely erased."

Customer: "Okay, I'm done. LOVE has started installing itself automatically. Is that normal?"

JC Rep: "Yes, it is. You should receive a message that says that LOVE is installed for the lifetime of your HEART. Do you see that message?"

Customer: "Yes. Is it completely installed?"

JC Rep: "Yes, but remember that you have only the basic program. You need to begin connecting to other HEARTS in order to get the upgrades."

Customer: "Oops. I have an error message already. What should I do?"

JC Rep: "What does the message say?"

Customer: "It says, 'ERROR 412 — PROGRAM NOT RUN ON INTERNAL COMPONENTS.' What does that mean?"

JC Rep: "Don't worry, ma'am. That is a common problem. It means that the LOVE program is set up to run on external HEARTS but has not yet been run on your HEART. It is one of those complicated programming things, but in non-technical terms it means you have to LOVE yourself before you can LOVE others."

Customer: "What should I do?"

JC Rep: "Can you find the directory called SELF-ACCEPTANCE?"

Customer: "Yes, I clicked SELF-ACCEPTANCE."

JC Rep: "You are getting good at this."

Customer: "Thank you."

JC Rep: "You are welcome. Click on the files and then copy them to MYHEART, FORGIVENESS, SELFESTEEM, REALIZE WORTH, and GOODNESS. The system will override any conflicting files and begin patching any faulty programming. Also, you need to delete SELFCRITIC from your directory and then empty your recycle bin afterwards to make sure it is completely gone and never comes back."

Customer: "Got it. Hey! My HEART is filling up with really neat files. SMILE, WARMTH, PEACE, and CONTENTMENT are copying themselves all over my HEART."

JC Rep: "Then LOVE has been installed and is running. Read John 3:16 to understand what has happened to you. One more thing."

Customer: "Yes?"

JC Rep: "LOVE is freeware. Be sure to give it and its various modules to everybody you meet. They in turn should share it with others. The JC Company assures you that as long as you get it and pass it on to others, that this installation will change your life."

We are sinners who need love and forgiveness. When we get this love and forgiveness from Jesus Christ, we can make an amazing confession. Dietrich Bonhoeffer made this insightful comment about the amazing confession in his book, *Life Together*:

> *Finally, one extreme thing must be said. To forego self-conceit and to associate with the lowly means, in all soberness and without mincing the matter, to consider oneself the greatest of sinners. This arouses all the resistance of the natural man but also that of the self-confident Christian. It sounds like an exaggeration, like an untruth. Yet even Paul said of himself that he was the foremost of sinners (1 Timothy 1:15); he said this specifically at the point where he was speaking of his service as an apostle. There can be no genuine acknowledgment of sin that does not lead to this extremity. If my sinfulness appears to me to be in any way smaller or less detestable in comparison with the sins of others, I am still not recognizing my sinfulness at all. My sin is of necessity the worst, the most grievous, the most reprehensible. Brotherly love will find any number of extenuations for the sins of others; only for my sin is there no apology whatsoever.*[6]

Think of it. Forgiveness from God means that I can find reasons for others' sins, but no rationalizations will do for my sins.

Think of it. I shouldn't consider my behavior horizontally, comparing it to others who may at first appear worse than me, but vertically with what God wants me to be so that I do indeed fall very short.

Think of it. Repentance means confessing sins of omission as well as commission, the secret sins which God sets in the light of his countenance.

Sin includes everything I have done wrong and, everything I have *not* done which I should have done.

Think of it and remember the hurt people, the lonely people, the insecure people, those at a distance, those close at hand, those unkind words, those unfair judgments.

Think of it and remember that we never catch up, we never cover our sins with our virtues, we never pay our debt. To be declared forgiven does not mean that you will never sin again, but that God knows how you are and still loves you. Luther said, "God covers you with forgiveness; he clothes you with his mercy."

Think of it. God wants sincerity in this petition. To pray, "Forgive us," without throwing your life behind the petition, is to make a mockery of the Lord's Prayer. If you expect God to take you seriously, you must take seriously your sinfulness, your tendency toward self-centeredness, your desire to be at the center with others at the edges of life. This is what the Bible calls sin.

A nice old woman came out of church one day after the pastor had been talking about sin. She complained to her pastor that she really didn't think she was all that bad. The real reason for her feelings, of course, was that she was judgmental about others and had not really taken her sin seriously. After some talk at the church door, she said to the pastor, "Well, if we are as bad as all that, God help us."

Precisely. That is what grace and forgiveness are all about.

Questions And Ideas
For Your Consideration And Discussion

1. Discuss the following statement: "Forgive us our sins as we forgive those who sin against us" is a kingdom of God petition. We can only begin to fulfill these words because Jesus ushered in the beginning of the kingdom, declared forgiveness from the cross, and empowers us to accept forgiveness and forgive others.

2. Discuss the computer representative of the JC Company in this chapter.

3. Discuss:

   Justice

   Mercy

   Grace

4. Consider the following thoughts about the Lord's Prayer:
   I can't really pray, "*Our*," if my faith has no room for others and their needs.
   I can't pray, "*Father*," if I don't demonstrate this relationship in my daily living.
   I can't pray, "*Who art in heaven*," if all my interests are in earthly things.
   I can't pray, "*Hallowed be thy name*," if I am unwilling to change or accept God's help to be holy.
   I can't pray, "*Thy kingdom come, thy will be done*," if I am unwilling to change or accept God's rule in my life.
   I can't pray, "*On earth as it is in heaven*," unless I am truly ready to give myself to God's service here and now.
   I can't pray, "*Give us this day our daily bread*," without expending honest effort for it; or if I would withhold from my neighbor the bread I receive.
   I can't pray, "*Forgive us our trespasses as we forgive those who trespass against us*," if I continue to harbor grudges against anyone.
   I can't pray, "*Lead us not into temptation*," if I deliberately choose to remain in situations where I am likely to be tempted.
   I can't pray, "*Deliver us from evil*," if I am not prepared to fight evil with my life and my prayer.
   I can't pray, "*Thine is the kingdom*," if I am unwilling to try to obey the King.
   I can't pray, "*Thine is the power and the glory*," if I am seeking power and glory for myself.

I can't pray, *"Forever and ever,"* if I am too anxious about each day's affairs.

I can't pray, *"Amen,"* unless I really mean what I pray.

— Anonymous

5. Consider Matthew 6:7-8: "And when you pray, do not keep on babbling like pagans, for they think they will be heard because of their many words. Do not be like them, for your Father knows what you need before you ask him."

Chapter 7

Save Us From The Great Ordeal And Deliver Us From The Evil One

A devout Christian woman once said to me, "I love the Lord's Prayer, but there is one thing in it which is confusing to me." "What is that?" I inquired. "It's that petition, 'Lead us not into temptation' " (Matthew 6:13), she said. That petition is confusing to a lot of people.

The traditional translation of the fifth petition is "Lead us not into temptation." The contemporary translation in *The Lutheran Book of Worship* is "Save us from the time of trial." As we look at the meaning of the fifth petition of the Lord's Prayer, the contemporary translation is helpful.

There are some substantial reasons to use the traditional version of the Lord's Prayer. This version is more familiar than the contemporary version. Dying people often pray the "Our Father" in the traditional language and find it very comforting. But there is at least one good reason to use the contemporary version. In the contemporary translation, the fifth petition of the Lord's Prayer is much closer to the original meaning than the traditional version. The Bible teaches that God tempts no person to sin. If God tempts no one to sin, why ask him not to lead us into temptation?

Save Us From The Time Of Trial

The Bible has many insights into the nature of temptation and trial. James 1:13-15 says:

> *When tempted, no one should say, "God is tempting me." For God cannot be tempted by evil, nor does he*

tempt anyone; but each one is tempted when by his own desire, he is dragged away and enticed. Then, after desire has conceived, it gives birth to sin; and sin, when it is full-grown, gives birth to death.

The book of Job teaches that the Tempter, not God, is the one who tempts us. Matthew 4:1 says that it was the Tempter who tempted Jesus in the wilderness. In both Job and Matthew 4:1, indeed throughout the Bible, God is pictured as the one who provides the means of escape from temptations and trials.

1 Corinthians 10:13 (RSV) says:

No temptation has overtaken you which is not common to man. God is faithful, and he will not let you be tempted beyond your strength, but with the temptation will also provide the means of escape, that you may be able to endure it.

Jesus in the high priestly prayer says:

My prayer is not that you take them out of the world but that you protect them from the Evil One.
— John 17:15

Theologians, basing their statements on the Bible, also emphasize that the Devil, not God, is the one who tempts us and that God is the one who saves us from temptations and trials.

In *The Small Catechism,* Martin Luther explains:

God tempts no one to sin, but we ask in this prayer that God would watch over us and keep us so that the devil, the world, and our sinful self may not deceive us and draw us into false belief, despair, and other great and shameful sins. And we pray that even though we are so tempted we may still win the final victory.[7]

Louis Evely, a Roman Catholic devotional writer, puts it this way: "The English translation 'And lead us not into temptation' is really blasphemous. As if God could wish to 'lead' us to do evil!"[8]

William Barclay, the New Testament scholar, points out that the Greek verb used in this fifth petition of the Lord's Prayer is *peirazein*. It should be translated "test" rather than "tempt" in the sense of seducing into evil. He points out, that it is God's intention to make us strong and thus save us when temptations and tests come.[9]

Helmut Thielicke, the German theologian, agrees that the petition is basically about God assisting us to overcome the Tempter and deliver us from the trials which come. " 'Oh, Lord, save us,' is a good translation," he says.[10]

Another good insight comes from Martin Niemoller, the German theologian who stood up to Adolf Hitler during World War II. Niemoller, who faced many trials and temptations, says that the meaning of this petition is that God leads no one *into* temptation or trials. God leads us through them. God gets us *through* the valleys of the shadows and saves us.

Most helpful of all, John V. Taylor, a New Testament scholar, translates the fifth petition in the light of the kingdom of God and Jesus' experience on the cross. He says that the best translation is "Save us from the Great Ordeal and deliver us from the Evil One."

Save Us From The Great Ordeal And Deliver Us From The Evil One

The Great Ordeal is the experience of the absence of God. Since Jesus ushered in the beginning of the kingdom of God and begins his prayer about the kingdom of God with the term of affectionate intimacy, *Abba*, we might expect that there would be no interruption of this relationship throughout his life. Instead, we find Jesus hanging on the cross at the end of his earthly life and feeling totally, utterly forsaken by his *Abba*. In juxtaposition to the intimacy of the first word of the Lord's Prayer, we find Jesus praying about being saved from the Great Ordeal in this petition. His struggle with the Evil One is real and profound throughout his life, but especially so as he hangs on the cross and appears to lose hope.

From the cross, Jesus cried out, "My God, my God, why have you forsaken me?" The feeling in the heart of darkness is that God has deserted us. That's what Jesus was talking about from the cross and in this petition of the Lord's Prayer. This is the time of trial, the Great Ordeal, when God who has always seemed so close that we could call him by the most intimate of names, *Abba*, seems so far away that we approach utter despair, suffering without hope.

In the Lord's Prayer, when Jesus prayed, "Save us from the Great Ordeal," he was talking about those times when we are tempted to give up, when we approach the great abyss of darkness and suffering and come close to believing that there is no longer any sense in believing that our *Abba* cares. Those are times when we feel utterly deserted, devoid, depressed, and desolate. In this petition we are being taught to pray, "Save us in those times when we are about to swallow the bait of the Tempter who wants us to believe that God is not there."

On Good Friday, Jesus carried the sins and burdens of all of us on his back at one point in time. He went to the heart of hell where people do not have hope. He went into the utter darkness so that we need never go there. Jesus blazed the trail through the heart of darkness so that we can see the light of God's presence, even when it seems that God does not care. Jesus prayed, "My God, my God, why have you forsaken me?" so that we need never swallow that demonic lure to give up on God.

As we pray this petition, we step away from what might be called "puppy sins" and look straight into the face of the monster sin of the Evil One, the Great Ordeal. In time of utter darkness, we are tempted to give up on God, who is our only hope. Through suffering, the Tempter lures us into thinking that we are utterly alone. We can come close to spiritual insanity losing contact with the only One who can help us.

In 1970, I stepped close to the edge of this spiritual insanity called the Great Ordeal when two friends and their two children died in a plane crash in Tampa, Florida. These friends, Lloyd and Bonnie Rhineschmidt, had volunteered to fly my wife Joyce and me in their private plane from Davenport, Iowa, to Sebring, Florida, where we had friends. Joyce had been sick with pneumonia. The doctor had said, "Get her to a warm climate where she can recover." The Rhineschmidts were taking a post-Christmas vacation in Tampa. "We will fly you to Sebring and then go on to Tampa," they said.

We got out of the plane in Sebring on December 31, 1969. The next day, January 1, 1970, we heard on the television news that six people had died in a plane crash at the Tampa airport. The passengers listed in the news included Lloyd and Bonnie Rhineschmidt, their two small children, and Ron and Joyce Lavin. The stop at Sebring and our departure had not been properly charted on the flight log. The television newscaster announced that we were dead. The newspaper headlines said the same thing. It was a soul-stirring thing to read and hear about our own deaths. It was even more soul-searching for me to realize that these four people were dead because they did us a favor by flying us to Sebring.

Then I went deeper into darkness when I was asked to preach at the funeral for the Rhineschmidts. What could I say to try to make sense out of these deaths when I could not see any sense in them myself?

This was the hardest funeral I have ever had. I was devastated. I was undone. I felt responsible for the deaths of four innocent people. My funeral sermon was empty because I was empty. My prayers bounced off the ceiling and back into my face. I felt that God had deserted me. Depression moved in like a fog. I could not get free from its demonic grip.

After several weeks of depression and moving about like a walking mummy, trying unsuccessfully to do my pastoral work, Bob Parker, the associate pastor at the church we served, came over to my house and said, "Ron, I would like to talk to you. You know that you are not responsible for the death of these four people."

"Yes," I said, "I know it in my mind, but the message has not yet reached my heart. If these people had not done us a favor by flying us to Sebring, they would still be alive today. How could this happen?"

"We don't know all the answers," he said, "but we do know that God is with us."

"I don't feel it," I said. "I know it in my *head*, but God's presence does not *feel* real."

Bob went on to explain that many Christians had experienced the dark night of the soul when God seems absent. He was very directive. "Get your mind on the cross of Jesus. Christ is here with us in our suffering," he said. I tried to picture Christ on the cross. "Now get down on your knees." I did. "Fold your hands." I did. "Pray the Lord's Prayer with me." I did. When we finished, Bob explained that God saves us in the times of the greatest ordeals by being with us. The words of Bob Parker, a voice beyond my own voices of torment, was the voice of God in the Great Ordeal. The Lord's Prayer and the petition about the Great Ordeal were the last thin string of hope which started my journey to recovery.

Christians, as well as pagans, sometimes get to the end of their rope, but Christians know a secret that one of my seminary professors taught me. The professor had lost a daughter in a fire. I asked him how he could go on. He replied, "When you get to the end of your rope, tie a knot and hang on. That is what faith means." When Bob Parker got me started on the road to recovery, I remembered the words of my professor, words that earlier I had forgotten to remember. "When you get to the end of your rope, tie a knot and hang on." These words helped to save me from the Great Ordeal and the Evil One.

I hope these stories will help you if ever you drop into the dark night of the soul. Two others may also help.

A Vanderbilt University religion student had been given the assignment by his professor to write the Lord's Prayer in his own words. The student was married and had a daughter who was suffering from a major joint problem. The little girl was not able to move her limbs. Her locomotion problem and the forthcoming surgery deeply depressed the young father. He started his version of the Lord's Prayer like this:

> *Our Father, who art in heaven,*
> *Why aren't you down here on earth,*
> *Doing something about my present difficulty?*
> *Who cares if your name is hallowed,*
> *Or whether or not your kingdom comes,*
> *When what concerns us most*

> *Is what life is really made of —*
> *Our big and little hurts?*

Then the student thought about the face of his little daughter. He also thought of the simple, pure faith she had in God. He imagined her talking to him about Jesus and his love. Crying into his typewriter keys, he again started on his assignment to write the Lord's Prayer in his own words. He wrote:

> *Our Father, in spite of the present difficulty,*
> *You are still in heaven and the world is still ordered.*
> *May my response hallow your name.*
> *The coming of your kingdom is more important than*
>   *my own difficulty*
> *So may I not hinder its coming by my worry.*
> *Cause this event to be an opening up to your will*
> *Which I can see as clearly as if I were in heaven.*
> *I must recognize that you still provide the necessities of*
>   *life*
> *I have bread enough.*
>
> *May this event help me to realize how important it is to*
>   *secure your forgiveness*
> *And may this not be an occasion for temptation to lose*
>   *faith or respond as a pagan.*
> *Deliver me from any evil response or action in this*
>   *difficulty.*
> *The overriding and all-important fact of life*
> *Is that to you belongs the kingdom and the power and*
>   *the glory forever.*

John Killinger, the teacher who received the personal paraphrase of the Lord's Prayer, writes this about the event:

> *A few days after the young man had come to this new viewpoint, the little girl was admitted to the hospital for her operation. I telephoned, thinking I would go to visit the parents during the surgery, but could not*

> locate them. *When I saw the young man again, I told him I had tried to reach him.*
> *He was all smiles. Apparently the operation had been deemed successful. "It was the strangest thing," he said. "They took our daughter for more x-rays the day before surgery was scheduled and her joint had started to grow. They didn't operate. The doctors said it was a miracle! Apparently she's going to be all right."*[11]

The Vanderbilt University student was lifted out of his dark night of the soul when he felt forsaken by God by imagining the face and faith of his child. Her words startled him back into the realization that he needed to be saved by his *Abba* at the very time he felt that he was forsaken by God. A child's voice was the voice of God. In another place with another man, a child's voice was the voice of *Abba*.

A seventeen-year-old believer named Ron Heagy found himself in the Great Ordeal. This young athlete was tempted to give up on God when he was hospitalized at Huntington Beach Community Hospital in California. He had broken his neck while swimming in the ocean at Huntington Beach. He was devastated by the realization that he could not move his arms or legs, but he kept hoping that this was a temporary condition and that through therapy, he would once again play football and be normal. The creeping realization that he would never walk or use his body in a normal way came over him late one night in the hospital. Sobbing in the darkness of the room, Ron cried out, "God, I can't go on. If I will never again be able to use my body, I don't want to live. I have loved you all of my life. Where are you now when I need you the most? I give up."

This is what the Great Ordeal is all about. Those who believe that God is near can suddenly find themselves in such suffering that they nearly lose hope. They approach the abyss of despair and are about to drop everything they have held dear. They get into the danger zone and nearly lose faith. This is what the Great Ordeal and the demonic forces named in this petition are all about. This is the danger zone. Our *Abba* does not seem to be there at all and the Tempter says, "Why not cut off contact with your heavenly Father? Who needs him? He has forsaken you." At these times we need to be delivered from the grasp of the Evil One. Ron experienced the Great Ordeal of nearly giving up on God. Ron was nearly swallowed up in despair.

Just then, Ron heard a child's voice. It was the voice of his eight-year-old roommate who had been paralyzed in a bike accident. The boy had been riding his bicycle and had been hit by a car. He had not been wearing a helmet. Since the accident, the eight-year-old had not spoken until this moment. "Ron," the boy said, "I love you. Don't give up. God is here. God will help you."

"That," said Ron Heagy, "was the turning point of my life. The voice of the child was the voice of God telling me to change my attitude." Today, Ron Heagy goes around the country in his electric wheel chair which he moves with his chin and tells his story, "Life Is An Attitude."[12]

Jesus said, "When you pray, say, '*Abba*, save us from the Great Ordeal and deliver us from the Evil One.'"

Questions And Ideas
For Your Consideration And Discussion

1. What is the Evil One trying to do to us in the Great Ordeal?

2. How has the Great Ordeal expressed itself in your life or in the life of someone you know?

3. Have you or someone you love heard the voice of God like that of Pastor Bob Parker, the daughter of the Vanderbilt student, or the eight-year-old in the story of Ron Heagy in this chapter?

Chapter 8

Your Glory

Yours is the kingdom and the power and the glory forever. Amen. — Matthew 6:13b

* * *

Does prayer really work? The Lord's Prayer flies right in the face of modern man's skepticism about prayer and his fear that it doesn't work. The Lord's Prayer is the model prayer. It was meant to teach us how to pray effectively if we put God at the center. In the Lord's Prayer we pray: "Hallowed be *your* name; *your* kingdom come; *your* will be done ... *yours* is the kingdom, the power and the glory forever."

That's the key which unlocks the mystery of effective prayer — centering on God. That's the meaning of the doxology — "Yours is the kingdom and the power and the glory forever." To *God* be the glory. To God be the *glory*.

To *God* Be The Glory

Prayer really works if we keep our eyes on the center of prayer which is God. People get confused about prayer and miss the power of prayer for many reasons. The main reason is that they do not put God in the center. Three mistakes emerge when people put themselves in the center: 1) they *say* the Lord's Prayer instead of *praying* it; 2) they regard prayer as magic to be used for human ends instead of a means of communication by which we give glory to God; and 3) they pray with a self-centered orientation instead of a God-centered attitude.

First, one of our problems with the Lord's Prayer is that we *say* it instead of *praying* it. To say our prayers costs us nothing. To pray means to center on God, to really believe in the One to whom you *pray*, not just *say* words. Just saying words means that we are not centering on God.

A chairperson of a church committee or council will often say, "Let us end the meeting by saying the Lord's Prayer." *Saying* the Lord's Prayer is different than *praying* it. In Matthew 6:1-8 Jesus told us to avoid being like the hypocrites who just *say* their prayers as an act of ritual or to be seen by others as being righteous.

In churches all over the world each Sunday pastors say: "Let us pray the Lord's Prayer." All too often people just *say* the prayer instead of *praying* it, because the words are so familiar. Just to *say* the Lord's Prayer is to recite it as a formula, the very thing Jesus warned us not to do in his introduction to the Lord's Prayer. Centering on God helps us to avoid vain repetitions in prayer which Jesus said are so dangerous. Praying "Our Father in heaven" with sincerity and thoughtfulness in communication with God is a way to stay in touch personally with our *Abba*. You wouldn't want your children to answer you with recorded messages. Neither does God want "canned," ritualistic, thoughtless repetitions from his children. To *say* the Lord's Prayer is to decentralize and depersonalize it.

I recently read that you can now buy an unusual telephone service in New York City. For a certain monthly charge you can have someone phone you every day and say, "I love you." What a strange depersonalized world we live in when people have to pay others to tell them that they are loved.

In this wonderland of gadgets, many people have forgotten how to belong personally to anyone, including God. This inability to belong and lack of personal relationships is at the heart of our modern problem with prayers. One reason we have trouble with prayer is because we have a tendency to make prayer a depersonalized recitation instead of a personal communication. *Abba* is a person to whom we pray. Therefore we *pray*, we do not just *say*, the Lord's Prayer.

Second, prayer is not autosuggestion or magic. Modern man is struggling with the need to get away from machines and activities and get in touch with himself. A recent magazine article suggested that a special time be set aside for daily prayer and meditation for the purpose of clarifying our ideas and composing our minds. But the article went on to say that of course modern people recognize there is no world beyond, no God to hear our prayers, no heavenly Father to understand our petitions. What a strange depersonalized world this is when we are told that prayer is only autosuggestion, when we are urged to pray to ourselves. To pray the Lord's Prayer means to communicate with our *Abba*.

A little boy was kneeling by the side of his bed saying his evening prayers, when his father entered the room. Turning to his father with a questioning look on his face, he said, "I know that I am transmitting, but I'm not sure that God is receiving." The boy's problem was that he was thinking of prayer as a way to get God to do what he wanted. That's a magical view of prayer which is understandable for a child, but inappropriate as we become mature Christians.

Can we really pray with confidence? Is prayer effective? Does God really hear us? Does he answer us? The Christian's answer to all of these questions is "Yes." We can pray with confidence if we keep God in the center and don't view prayer as autosuggestion or magic.

You may remember Huckleberry Finn's account of prayer and how he stopped praying when it didn't produce the results he wanted:

> *Miss Watson she took me into the closet, and prayed but nothing come of it. She told me to pray every day, and whatever I asked for I would get it. But it warn't so. I tried it. Once I got a fish line but no hooks. I tried for hooks three or four times, but somehow I couldn't make it work.*

Poor old Huck! He made the same mistake a lot of us make. He got prayer confused with magic. Prayer is the process whereby we open ourselves up to discover the will of God so we can do and be what he wants. Magic, on the other hand, is the process of trying to manipulate God so he will do what we want.

Prayer is not autosuggestion or magic that gets us what we want or think we need, ignoring the most important ingredient in prayer — the glory of God. The doxology is a marvelous biblical corrective for a depersonalized *saying* of prayers as if they were magic to attain our personal ends. Prayer is not a matter of trying to get what we want from God, but getting tuned into what God wants. God is seeking to communicate to us. Prayer means asking God: "What will glorify your name?"

Third, true prayer is an expression of God-centeredness, not self-centeredness. To pray the doxology means that we lose ourselves in God, not try to get something from God. A little girl was asked by her mother why she had slipped into bed without saying her prayers. "There are some nights," she replied, "when I don't want anything." The purpose to prayer is to tune into what God has for us. Tuning into God's station means that we are seeking God's glory in our lives.

What does it mean to pray to God's glory? That is *the* question raised by the doxology.

To God Be The *Glory*

The doxology is not in the earliest manuscripts of the Gospel of Saint Matthew and Saint Luke, the two Gospels that contain the Lord's Prayer. That is why it appears as a footnote in most translations. It was likely a liturgical addition which the early Christians used when they prayed the prayer which Jesus had taught them, but what a magnificent and appropriate addition it is! Like a second bookend, combining with the emphasis on God's name in the opening petition, it takes our attention to the heart of the matter: God's glory. Prayer is not a matter of trying to get something from the Father, but exposing yourself to the Father's will and ways, to his kingdom, his power, and his glory.

Modern man has lost his sense of respect for God. Going on his own self-centered way, caught up in his "own thing," modern man has lost respect for himself, his neighbor, and his Maker. Does that have to be illustrated? How many times this week will you be confronted by discourteous drivers, discourteous shoppers, discourteous customers or salespersons? How many discourtesies will be experienced in your own home this week? This epidemic of discourtesy is reversed as we pray the doxology and thus restore our respect and love for God, get caught up in the wonder of self-forgetfulness before God, and enter the wonderful world of the glory of God. Consider three aspects of the glory of God.

First, to give God the glory means respecting and adoring the One we say we love. The doxology calls us to return love to God in prayer, because he first loved us. Loving God and people is the one thing needful and the hardest thing of all.

The Hebrew word that we translate "glory" is *shekinah*. *Shekinah* means God's personal presence on earth. We love God back when we discover the personal presence of God. The brightness of the heavenly Father shines in the darkness to those whose eyes are open to behold it. That's why we love and adore the Lord in prayer. In the person of Jesus, God's love for us shines. The Gospel of John reports:

> *The Word became flesh and made his dwelling among us. We have seen his glory, the glory of the One and only, who came from the Father, full of grace and truth.*
> — John 1:14

The doxology teaches us to center our love on God's glory in his Son, our Savior. "Yours is the glory," we pray, centering our prayers on God, not self.

Second, to give glory to God is a step into the wonderful world of self-forgetfulness. When you love someone, you think of him or her first, not yourself. When you love God because he first loved you, you forget yourself and enjoy the kingdom of God, God's rule over us for our own good. Love is not easy, of course, since it means going outside of ourselves. John 3:16 says, "God so loved the world that he gave his only begotten Son...."

In a *Peanuts* cartoon I recently saw, Charlie Brown and Lucy are engaged in conversation. Lucy's back is turned, her arms are folded, and a look of disgust appears on her face. Charlie is pleading, as usual, for her to be tolerant and understanding. With outstretched arms he says:

> *"Lucy, you must be loving. This world really needs love. You have to let yourself love to make this world a better place in which to live!"*
> *Lucy whirls around and screams (as Charlie does his famous back flip): "Look, blockhead – the world I love. It's people I can't stand!"*

The Lord's Prayer teaches us to love people by teaching us to pray, "Forgive us our sins as we forgive those who sin against us." It also teaches us to love God by teaching us to pray, "Yours is the kingdom, the power, and the glory." We love God with self-forgetfulness for all he has done. Think of the cross and you will realize how much God loves you.

In his devotional book *My Utmost For His Highest*, Oswald Chambers urges us to surrender our wills to God and stretch out our response to God who has stretched out to us with grace in the cross. When we survey the cross, we will know the truth of the old hymn, "Were the whole realm of glory mine, that were an offering far too small. Love so amazing, so divine, demands my soul, my life my all." In that song we stretch out in response to what God has done for us in Jesus Christ. We offer our utmost for God's highest. We enter the realm of self-forgetfulness.

The Lord's Prayer is all about loving and glorifying God with self-forgetfulness. "Hallowed be your name (Your name is holy) ... Your kingdom come ... Your will be done ... Yours is the kingdom, the power and the glory." These prayer petitions center us on God, not ourselves. These prayer petitions are all about God's kingdom and glory.

To love God and his kingdom with self-forgetfulness means to realize that the world belongs to God — not to the wealthy, not to the mighty, not to the successful, but to God. The kingdom, the power and the glory are God's, not man's.

Third, to give glory to God puts us in touch with the heart of prayer which is praise. Thus the Lord's Prayer comes to its close with a great burst of praise and joy with the words, "for yours is the kingdom, the power, and the glory." Empires perish, but God's kingdom is forever. Powerful people all suffer and die, but God's power is everlasting. Praise for people comes crashing down when they disappoint us, but praise of God rises like a sweet smelling offering to the throne of God. Have our hearts grown too weary, our ears too dull, our lives too complacent to be aroused by the great adventure of the kingdom of God and the praise of the Almighty? It is an adventure in self-forgetfulness.

Modern man has great difficulty with love, self-forgetfulness, and praise because he is caught in the trap of the "Me Generation." One of the most popular trends of today is a glorification of self and selfishness, despite the consequences such actions have for us and other people. The 1970s were dubbed the years of the "Me Generation" by author Tom Wolfe. He coined the phrase to indicate the "me first" attitude among a growing number of people. The 1980s and 1990s and the beginning of the 21st century have continued and extended the trend of selfishness!

In other words, the old American way of pulling together, helping each other, extending a hand to people less fortunate has vanished for many people in the "Me Generation." The spirit of television's Waltons, of the American pioneers, of World War II, of people helping people has no place with the "me first" group. Praise of God is the opposite of the "me first" attitude.

We see this "me first" attitude all around us. Look at today's books, magazines, and movies. The "me first" attitude is also seen in the vanishing interest in politics, in the declining number of people who vote, and in decreasing interest in grass-roots organizing to change our society for the better. In other words, people in the "Me Generation" could care less about anyone else other than themselves. This trend is unhealthy for individuals and society. Self-centeredness results in passing trash around to others.

A six-year-old boy was overheard praying the Lord's Prayer at a church service. "And forgive us our trash passes as we forgive those who pass trash against us."[13] That's the prayer of egotistical sinners caught up in the trash of a "me first" attitude of egotists.

Egotists don't praise God. George Goldtrap describes an egotist as "someone who is *me* deep in conversation."[14]

Love for God, self-forgetfulness, and praise of God have long been the cornerstone of Christianity. This is the secret of the Christian life, a secret that many people have yet to discover. We *say* over and over again, "Yours is the glory," but sometimes we don't think of what that really means. It means love, self-forgetfulness, and praise.

Praise is the heart of our faith. The Lord's Prayer ends with praise. The praise of God is a perspective from which all good things come. The mysteries of the kingdom of God cannot be comprehended by an outsider, because everything in the kingdom depends on the praise perspective. We never learn how mighty, powerful, and glorious the kingdom of God is until we try to live as kingdom people. Kingdom people center prayers on praise. To praise God is to see life from the special perspective of heaven. True worship is adoration, self-forgetfulness, and praise. Prayer is praise more than it is anything else.

A Christian man had great difficulty with his fleshly passions. He prayed over and over, "O Lord, deliver me from my passions and forgive me for my lust and the many times I have committed adultery," but he continued to be possessed by sexual desires which were out of control until he learned the secret of prayer. He had been so preoccupied with his sinfulness that he had overlooked the most important thing of all — God's glory. Even in fighting his sin he was too involved in it and thus fell into sin time after time. He prayed over and over, "Lord, deliver me from my problem of lust," until one day he discovered the secret of Christian prayer when he prayed: "Lord, I thank you for my sexuality, a great gift of your creation which you have given me. Help me to use it to your glory and honor." The spell of lust was broken by shifting his prayers from his problems to praising God. He shifted from the negative to the positive. That's what self-forgetful praise means.

Another man tells of his ability to be calm and composed during the air raids of World War II. He came to discover the secret of praising God. He found that when he thought about the bombs and prayed for deliverance for himself and his family, he remained in a state of high tension and anxiety, but when he began to praise and thank God for the safety and salvation he provided — when he focused on the glory of God — he knew an inner peace. That's what the doxology invites us to do — focus our attention on God's glory. The man learned the secret of the Lord's Prayer, praising God: "Yours is the kingdom, the power and the glory...."

Saint Paul sang praises to God at midnight from jail (Acts 16:25). He knew the secret of praise. Despite the obvious circumstances of the stench of prison, the rats, and the bad company; the injustice of being arrested and mistreated though his only crime was telling people about God; despite his weary bones and mind which had come as a result of so many refusing to understand the wonder of faith — despite it all, Saint Paul sang psalms and praises to God in the darkness of his prison cell. That's what the doxology is all about.

Prayer is not primarily petitions for what we want or think we need. Prayer is not even primarily intercessions for others in need, as important as that is. Prayer is primarily praise as the magnificent doxology teaches us. The Lord's Prayer ends as it began — centered on God. "Our heavenly *Abba* ... Yours is the kingdom and the power and the glory forever. Amen." The doxology is a paean of praise to God which breaks forth when we are overwhelmed by God's love and grace.

The biblical corrective for a self-seeking "Me Generation" caught in the trap of disrespect, depersonalization, and self-centeredness is the restoration of the doxology to our prayers and to our lives. Prayer really works when we discover this secret.

The Lord's Prayer is all about the kingdom, the power, and the glory of God. We will not experience that kingdom in fullness until we die or the end of the world comes, but we get glimpses of it when we pray in harmony with the secret of prayer which is centering on God, his power and his glory.

To *God* be the glory. To God *be* the glory. To God be the *glory* for the things he has done.

Questions And Ideas
For Your Consideration And Discussion

Fill in the blanks and discuss.

1. The meaning of God's glory is _____
   _____

2. Modern man has lost his respect for _____
   _____

3. The secret of effective prayer as taught in the Lord's Prayer is
   _____

Endnotes

Chapter Two
1. Martin Luther, *The Small Catechism* (Minneapolis: Augsburg, 1979), p. 17.

Chapter Four
2. John Thomas Randolf, *Lord Teach Us To Pray* (Lima, Ohio: CSS Publishing Company, 1977), pp. 32-37.

3. Helmut Thielicke, *Our Heavenly Father* (New York: Harper and Row, 1960), p. 75.

Chapter Five
4. Jesus often spoke in Aramaic, a dialect of Hebrew. The earliest Greek manuscripts use the Greek word *epiousion*, which we translate "food for sustenance." *Machar* (the Aramaic word Jesus probably used) means "tomorrow's bread today," as many translations indicate in footnotes on this passage.

5. Henri Nouwen, *With Open Hands* (New York: Ballantine Books, 1972), p. 79.

Chapter Six
6. Dietrich Bonhoeffer, *Life Together*, tr. John Doberstein (New York: Harper, 1954), p. 96.

Chapter Seven
7. Luther, *op. cit.*, p. 21.

8. Louis Evely, *We Dare To Say Our Father*, 10th Impression (New York: Herder and Herder, 1966), p. 110.

9. William Barclay, *The Gospel of Matthew*, Vol. 1, 2nd edition (Philadelphia: The Westminster Press, 1968), pp. 225-227.

10. Helmut Thielicke, *Our Heavenly Father*, tr. John Doberstein (New York: Harper & Bros., 1960), pp. 115-145.

11. John Killinger, *Bread for the Wilderness; Wine for the Journey* (Waco, Texas: Word Books, 1978), pp. 52-53.

12. Ron Heagy, *Life Is An Attitude* (Multnomah, 1997).

Chapter Eight

13. Cal and Rose Samra, *More Holy Humor* (Carmel, New York, 1997), p. 37.

14. *Ibid.*, p. 67.

Tips For Teachers, Pastors, And Leaders

1. This book may be used in Sunday school classes for adults or teenagers. It may also be used for small groups meeting in the homes of members or at the churches.

2. You may want to use the questions at the end of each chapter for discussion starters. You may want to use other questions that you think of. Use whatever works for you and your group.

3. **Remember, you are a leader, not a lecturer. Your job is to draw out the answers to questions from the people.**

4. It is sometimes helpful to break into groups of two people to discuss the questions to assure that everyone participates. Then you can have each group of two report in to the whole group.

5. My book, *Way To Grow! Dynamic Growth Through Small Groups*, is about several models for small groups and the ways and means to get groups going and keep them going. The books, *I Believe; Help My Unbelief* (on the Apostles' Creed), *Stories To Remember* (on Jesus' Parables), and *Turning Griping Into Gratitude* (on the Psalms), are also designed as study books for groups. They are available from CSS Publishing Company, P. O. Box 4503, Lima, Ohio 45804-4503. Phone orders can be made to: 1-800-537-1030. FAX: 1-419-228-9184 or e-mail: orders@csspub.com Other recommended books for study are listed on page 4 of this book.

6. Each participant in a group which discusses *Abba* should have a copy of the book. To order, contact CSS Publishing Company as indicated in note 5 above. To order books for your group, have CSS bill your church or you personally; then distribute the books, collect the money from participants, and pay the bill.

Appendix #1

A Mother's View Of The Lord's Prayer

Mary Lavin Cousler

When my dad (Ron Lavin) first approached me with the idea of writing an appendix for this book I thought, "What could *I* share about the Lord's Prayer?" I'm a stay-at-home mother of three boys, with a background in natural resource management and creative writing, characteristics that in no way qualify me to share a theological opinion about the Lord's Prayer.

However, after much thought and introspection, it occurred to me that as a Christian, I am not only qualified, but actually called to share the gospel in every way, shape, and form possible. I don't need to be a theologian to share my personal experiences, reflections, and love of the Lord. With these thoughts in mind, let me proceed with some impressions of the Lord's Prayer, *from a mother's heart.*

"Our Father in heaven ..."

One of the greatest joys of being a mother is having a chance to view the world from a child's perspective. Everything looks different through their eyes. Take, for instance, the concept of God, the Father, who is here with us, yet also in heaven; the Great I AM who was, is, and always shall be. How in the world do you explain that concept to a kindergartner? You wait for an opening ...

"Mommy, how old is God?" asked our son, Jimmy, who was then six years old. I enthusiastically replied that God was *very* old. In fact, he was older than anybody or anything. Jimmy was quiet for a minute. Then he asked, "Mom, is he even older than the *dinosaurs*?" I replied, "Why, yes, he is. Much older." Jimmy sat there silently, his little forehead furrowed in deep thought. I could tell that my answer did not fully satisfy his inquiring mind. I wanted to see what would happen next so I held back the impulse to keep talking. After a long pause, his face lit up and he said confidently, "Wow. He must be forty." Well ... so much for bridging the generation gap!

God is old, older than time itself. God is strong, stronger than all the forces of nature combined. God is big, bigger than the whole universe. Yet God knows each of us intimately and cares for us as his children. How is that possible? God reached down through the ages, through time and space, and connected with us in the form of Jesus, the Christ. Jesus, in turn, taught us to reconnect with our God, our source, our creator when he taught us to pray, "Abba, Our Father, who are in heaven, hallowed be your name."

*"**Your** kingdom come, **your** will be done ..."* (emphasis mine).

I always notice how the Lord's Prayer says *your* will rather than *my* will. The human will is a formidable thing, especially the will of a spirited three-year-old boy ...

When our middle son, Stevie, was three he had a black Batman t-shirt. It was his favorite. He would have worn it all day, every day had I not intervened and insisted that it be given a rest (and a wash) once or twice a week. One night after his bath, he saw this favorite shirt rumpled in a pile of soon-to-be-washed clothes. I had chosen a fresh pair of pajamas for him, but he really wanted to wear that shirt. I calmly explained to him that the shirt was dirty and he was going to have to wear something else. He angrily crossed his little arms and said, "No. I want *that* one." I kept my cool and repeated, "Honey, the shirt is dirty. You need to put on these pajamas."

More determined than ever now, he stomped his foot and pointed to the shirt on the floor and said, "NO! I want THAT one!" Nearing my limit of patience, I looked him straight in the eye, and rebutted, "Steve, the answer is no, and when Mommy says, 'No,' NO means NO." He never batted an eye. Defiantly placing his hands squarely on his hips, he declared, "Yes means YES!" I couldn't keep myself from laughing at this boy who would be king!

God wants us to express all of our needs and desires to him through prayer. But that doesn't automatically mean that we get whatever we pray for. I've heard people say from time to time that prayer doesn't work. After all, they go on, they prayed for something that didn't come to pass. Perhaps the Lord heard their prayers, but they just didn't like his answer!

Jesus taught us that we are to come before the Lord, not to try to bend God's will for our purposes. Rather, we are to seek out *his* will in prayer, then unquestioningly do it, "on earth as it is in heaven."

"Give us this day our daily bread ..."

We try to teach our children to be thankful to God for what they receive, including the gift of daily food. That means trying to teach them to say, "Thank you," at meals. When they forgot to pray at meals, we worked on the project of gratefulness by asking, "What are the 'magic words'?"

One day Jimmy was particularly stubborn about his determination to get to the food without bothering to pray. "What are the magic words?" I asked.

"Now," he replied with determination. "I want to eat now."

Whoops. Back to the drawing board.

"... and forgive us our sins as we forgive those who sin against us ..."

One afternoon not long ago, I was reviewing an article I had written for our church's newsletter. Being a little pressed for time, I needed a few minutes to finish the piece. I put on a video for the children to watch, hoping to buy myself some time at the computer. The minute I started typing there was a loud scuffle in the next room, instantly followed by crying. I investigated quickly. Our youngest son, Tom, tearfully pointed to Stevie and said, "Mommy, he hit me!" Turning my attention to the suspect, I said with concern in my voice, "Steve, did you hit Tom?" He answered a brief, "Yep," never taking his eyes off of the movie. So I stepped in front of the television set to gain his full attention. "Oh, Honey, *why* did you hit Tom?" I asked, perturbed. Stevie looked at me puzzled, as if I should have known the answer to such an obvious question, and responded nonchalantly, "Well, he hit me first!" So much for turning the other cheek.

Everyone has been wronged at one time or another, either intentionally or unintentionally. Yet it is our response to that injury that defines our character. Who hasn't heard the phrase, "To err is human, to forgive, divine." I've also heard it put this way, "To err is human, to forgive ... impossible!" That may be a truer reflection of our society than we want to admit! If it is true that God forgives us in the *exact* same manner that we forgive others, how can we *ever* hope to gain salvation? There is only one way: through God's grace, and the sacrifice that his only son made for us on Calvary.

"Save us from the time of trial ..."

September 11, 2001, is a day that will be forever etched into the souls of the American people. Millions watched the story unfold like some terrible scene from an over-dramatized disaster movie.

My husband Greg has been a fireman since 1988 in Las Cruses, New Mexico. He was at work that day, so I was at home alone with the boys. I watched in horror as the World Trade towers collapsed, knowing with certainty that thousands of people had just died. I sat sobbing on the couch, completely consumed with grief for the firemen, police officers, and businessmen and women who were in those buildings. Puzzled by my behavior, Stevie wandered up to me and asked, "What's wrong, Mama?" I managed to choke out the words, "Oh, Honey ... those buildings were full of people ... the buildings just fell and all of those people died." I held him close and wept.

I knew that we had to pray. I gathered both Tom and Stevie on to my lap and we prayed together for all of the people who had just died and for their families. We also prayed for the souls of those responsible for taking the lives of so many people that morning. When we were finished, I gave them each a big hug and sent them outside to play.

After a while, Stevie came back inside, and seeing me still upset by the events of the day, he said, "Mommy, we should pray again." I nodded to him, unable to speak. He folded his little hands over mine and began, "Dear God, help all the people be okay, help their families ... and forgive the bad guys, too ... Amen."

Where is God in our times of trial? Are we abandoned to our own suffering and despair? No, he has promised that he will always be with us and we will never be alone. If we keep looking, we will find that he is here with us even now, and that he has been right beside us all along. Sometimes God even appears in the form of a child.

"For the kingdom, the power, and the glory are yours, now and forever. Amen."

Greg's job as a firefighter prohibits him from being home every evening, so we make the most of the time we have. We try to have meals together as often as we can, and always say a prayer before each meal begins. The boys' favorite one is: "God is great, God is good, and we thank him for our food. Amen." Short, sweet, to the point, let's eat!

One evening when Greg was home, we gathered at the table for dinner. The children had behaved themselves particularly well that day, and we were all in a good humor as we sat down. Greg helped Stevie into his chair, and putting his arm around him, asked him to say the prayer for the family. Always ready to put on a show for us, Stevie gladly obliged and said in a loud voice, "God is GRRREAT! Aaaa-men!" We all laughed and enjoyed a wonderful evening together.

Life is often a mixture of triumph and tragedy, of joy and sadness, of monotony and purpose. But through it all, God's love is ever-present. Even though we mess up, he forgives us. Even though we reject him, he still loves us. Even though we didn't deserve it, he sent his son to show us the way back to him. That's just amazing, isn't it? You know what, Stevie? You were right. God is GRRREAT! Aaaaa-men!

Soli Deo Gloria

Appendix #2

My Journey

Carol Lewis

Reflecting on my journey towards God brings to mind Paul McCartney's voice singing, "The long and winding road...." There have been times I have seen the road straight ahead of me clearly, and times when I perceived my map was unreliable and had to change directions. Later, I would be moved back onto the road with new vigor and trust, only to begin to daydream and veer off again. I was learning to drive. Thanks to the Lord of all, now I have my permanent license! Some of us need more practice than others.

The first steps on the path of faith began during my adolescent years, while I was happily well-grounded in rock and roll, looking for boys, and having the most fun possible. A new pastor had arrived in my town of Lebanon, Indiana. A friend of mine gave him my name as an "unchurched teen." The last thing I wanted was a visit from some preacher, so I actively avoided Pastor Ron Lavin for as long as possible, but to no avail. God sent his unrelenting servant into my life. He felt the call to nudge me down the road he was traveling, the road to God.

I don't recall the details of the evening he caught up to me at my home, but I am ever amazed at the outcome of the meeting. I reluctantly agreed to meet him and the dozen or so other teenagers he had recruited for what he called a confirmation class. Life changed with additions of Saturday morning classes, Bible study worksheets for homework, weekly worship, Sunday school classes, and sermon condensations for the man we affectionately called "Pastor Baby."

In addition, I joined the youth choir, directed by Ron's wife Joyce. Joyce had phenomenal patience with the immature, giggling, adolescent girls. "Pastor Baby" and Joyce were God's secret weapons to find us, teach us, and lead us on the paths of righteousness. Other adults at Trinity Lutheran Church taught our Sunday school class and led our youth group. They could all be counted on to *be there when needed.* These dedicated people not only showed up for us, they made us feel loved, even when we were pretty sure we weren't very lovable. In this little mission church I was beginning to see a reflection of the glorious love God gives through his people.

Pastor Ron also demonstrated his love for me by paying attention to what was really happening in my life and what he wanted me to avoid. He was able to communicate his concerns clearly while building my self-esteem with his unexpected belief in my potential. This was a new experience for me. I was learning about fatherly care and concern. I had heard stories about loving fathers, but my experiences taught me I did not deserve a father like that. God gave Pastor Ron insights beyond his young age of 24. He "fathered" me into the faith.

At the end of that first year of my Christian journey, I was baptized and confirmed. I was walking along the road to our heavenly Father. I had been pointed in the right direction and I had taken a few baby steps along the right path. The spiritual part of me wanted to stay the course, but there was another voice in my head. The rebellious side of me wanted to assert that I was really in control of my own life and nobody, not even God, was going to take over. I remained very active in my church throughout high school and therefore held on to my fledgling faith, even through the times of doubting.

The college years were another story. Ron and Joyce encouraged me to attend Ball State University in Muncie, Indiana. They had moved to Muncie during my senior year in high school. They had vision and motivation for me which was beyond my limited view of the world. In our family, graduating from high school and not getting pregnant before marriage was considered a major achievement. College? No way. Not enough brains. No money. To me, the idea of college was laughable. "I'm too dumb," I said. "And there is no money."

"You aren't dumb. If we can get you the money, will you come?" they asked.

"Yes, but it will never happen."

Free room and board with professors at Ball State, a scholarship based on need, and a part time job were arranged for me. I went to college with $20 in my pocket. Ron and Joyce were showing me again what God was like. With no little embarrassment I admit I was a little slow to get it. Even with all of these signs of divine guidance, college brought out the doubting side of my mind.

During the college years I stopped going to church. A philosophy professor challenged the class to make him a believer in Christianity by proving that some virgin gave birth to a baby who was the Son of God. My mind became fertile ground for the lies of the Enemy. My spiritual journey came to a screeching halt.

Ron and Joyce stuck by me. They tried to influence me to see Christianity for what it really is, but my mind was fixed. They let me know they respected my honest questioning and no matter what, they would always consider me a part of their family. Through their actions, they showed what God the Father is like. Ron and Joyce and God, my Father, never abandoned me, even when I was rebellious. It was a proud day for all of us when I graduated from Ball State in deaf education.

At age 24, I married Hugh Lewis, another teacher of the deaf. He was a lifelong Christian. Ron married us in the little church in Lebanon where I had met him as a teenager. Through the first years of our marriage, Hugh remained faithful, attending church regularly. He waited for me to have a change of heart. My agnostic mindset continued for about five years. Then a slow realization came upon me. My Christian friends and loved ones possessed a peace and assurance I wanted.

One night, lying in bed thinking about the situation, I recalled the words of my spiritual father, Ron. "If you want to believe, but can't feel it, just act as if you already believe and change will come. More people act themselves into right ways of thinking than think themselves into right ways of acting." I prayed to God (even though

I wasn't sure there was a God). I asked God (if he existed) to let me know how to have the faith I couldn't intellectually accept at that point. Within seconds, I had a revelation that still brings tears to my eyes and goose bumps to my body and soul. It felt like the hour I first believed. I saw a mental vision of the face of Christ and heard the words, "I am the one who has been pulling you along all this time."

While those words might not mean anything to someone else, they were specifically meant for me. I understood immediately that this was God. In a split second Christ broke through all the rebellion and mistrust that had trashed my spirit for years. Why had I not seen it sooner? I had been "pulled along" by the mighty force of the Lord. Since that revelation, I have never lost belief in who God is.

The next dozen or so years were spent in intense church work. I felt a specific calling to work with adolescents, because of the powerful experiences I had through the love of Christian adults when I was young. God gave me gifts to connect with kids, a ministry filled with great joy, satisfaction, and responsibility. *And disappointment.*

Church work isn't always easy. Hugh and I were both working as deaf educators and trying to raise our two sons while trying to work hard in the church. I was staying connected with Christian friends, learning more about how to live a Christian life, and using my spiritual gifts in the work of the Lord. But the load was heavy on this journey. When I looked honestly at some of the leaders of our church, some of the members and the game called "church politics," my old nemesis of doubt began to reappear.

Negative feelings were building up within me. The straw that broke the camel's back was the decision by church leaders to reduce substantially the amount of money given to youth work at our church, even though youth ministry was very effective. Frustrated and exhausted, I abruptly stopped attending church. I had hit a brick wall on the long, winding road.

Over the next ten years, I stopped paying attention to my faith, instead nurturing my passion for theater, music, and traveling. These passions diminished over time. Nothing I did satisfied my longings.

I blamed my husband (poor Hugh, always my first target), my job, my age, and a wide variety of other factors, but blame didn't satisfy. I was an unhappy drifter on the road of life.

While heading for the home decorating section of the Barnes and Noble book store in our town (St. Augustine, Florida), I was pulled by an invisible hand to the religion section. There was no conscious motivation to go there. Inexplicably I picked up *Mere Christianity* by C. S. Lewis (no relative). Out of curiosity, I purchased the book. As I read Lewis, I had an epiphany or revelation — call it what you will. I said, "Yes," as I read, "we are responsible to take care of the faith we are given through discipline, not just feelings. Our will is what God cares about, not just feelings. The natural self must die. Yet we can't accomplish this ourselves. It is a part of what God does for us on the journey of faith."

I was so moved by the clarity of vision in Lewis' words, I reread the book two more times, highlighting more each time. I was hooked.

Then someone suggested that I attend a little Episcopal church nearby. I was tempted to say, "No." It is hard to enter a church where you don't know anyone. The words of C. S. Lewis rang in my mind. "The Enemy wants to keep us away from taking care of the faith we have. The Enemy will supply endless excuses to keep us from church." I went. Then I went again.

There was a pull to this little church I could not explain. The church had a mix of ages and races. The mix of traditional and contemporary music fed me. The love of the pastor was radiant. The members loved one another. The authentic neighborhood ministries attracted me. There was vision there. And God was there.

As I pray for guidance to discover my role in this church, I not only worship regularly, I also attend a Bible study group. I am praying with renewed awareness.

Finally, I get it. Finally, after all these years, I am filled with joy and thankfulness to my heavenly Father. Finally, our Father's love and faithfulness to me, an unworthy follower, has dawned on me like a bright new day. Finally, after all these struggles, I am again on the long, winding road, the road that leads home to my real Father, our Abba.

Thirty-five years ago, when I was in the grip of doubt and agnosticism, Joyce Lavin wrote me a letter saying that when I finally accepted and trusted God, I would speed down the road of faith as if in a shiny red convertible. She added, "Just don't forget to fill 'er up!"

Thanks, Joyce. The tank is overflowing with joy and gratefulness.

www.ingramcontent.com/pod-product-compliance
Lightning Source LLC
Chambersburg PA
CBHW071723040426
42446CB00011B/2186